THE CENTURY OF PRINT

# bauhausbücher

# 12

editors:
walter gropius
l. moholy-nagy

walter gropius

# bauhaus buildings dessau

walter gropius

# bauhaus buildings dessau

lars müller publishers

Originally published in German under the title of
"Bauhausbauten Dessau" by Albert Langen Verlag München
in 1930, printed by Hesse & Becker Leipzig, printing blocks
by C. Dünnhaupt GmbH Dessau.
First English edition published by Lars Müller, based on
the first German edition. Translation by Helen Ferguson.

ISBN 978-3-03778-665-9
Printed in Germany
www.lars-mueller-publishers.com


printing: dza druckerei zu altenburg
reproduction: integral lars müller / zurich
typography, cover, jacket:
l. moholy-nagy / berlin

# contents

# preface

this book is a report — about a now concluded, fruitful period of construction, development and shared work.

the history of the bauhaus begins in weimar in spring 1919. appointed by the provisional government in saxony-weimar-eisenach, i took over as director of the former "großherzogliche hochschule für bildende kunst" and the former "großherzogliche kunstgewerbeschule" founded by van de velde. with the government's consent, i named the new comprehensive institute "staatliches bauhaus in weimar." the basic aim of the bauhaus was to synthesize all artistic creation into a unified whole, to unite all artistic and technical disciplines into a new art of architecture as their indissoluble components, an art of architecture at the service of a vibrant life.

after the war brutally interrupted the work, the need for change became pressing for every thinking person. everyone longed to bridge the fatal gap between reality and spirit. this desire came together in the bauhaus.

many talented young people looked to the manifesto for establishment of the bauhaus to devote themselves to the bauhaus's far-reaching social role in a time of immense economic deprivation and in the face of a harsh enemy in an uncomprehending environment. overcoming its own mistakes and always full of the greatest vitality, the bauhaus gradually found its way. it slowly clarified matters for itself in a struggle against the formalistic views of the time. clear, seemingly self-evident ideas take the longest to become reality because of their radical, i.e. deep-rooted origins, which makes them valid not just for one narrow, easily overlooked area but for life in general. with all the methods of conceptual interpretation and synthetic understanding, the bauhaus set out with tenacious energy to get to the roots of the problem of design and to make everyone aware of the results of its realizations, namely: that artistic design must not be a spiritual or material luxury, but a matter of life itself! that, furthermore, the revolution of the artistic spirit brought elementary insights for the new design, just as the technical revolution brought the tools for its fulfillment! all efforts were directed toward advancing into both groups of the spirit, liberating creative human beings from their seclusion from the world by connecting them with the salutary realities of the world of work and at the same time loosening and expanding the rigid, narrow, almost solely material focus of the economy. this social idea of the unity of all creative work in its relationship to life itself — in contrast to "l'art pour l'art," as well as to its riskier cause, "the economy as an end in itself" — thus dominated the bauhaus's work. the direction it adopted was initially more decisive than the results produced during the early period.

the bauhaus's passionate participation in this intellectual debate is the source of its keen interest in the design of technical products and organic development of their production methods, which led to the erroneous view that it was establishing an apotheosis of rationalism. it sought instead to define the shared conditions and limitations of the realm of creativity in the design and technical fields: "each thing is determined by its essence. in order to ensure it functions properly, its essence must be explored, for it must serve its purpose to the full, i.e. fulfill its functions practically, as well as being durable, cheap and 'beautiful'"; ●) however the smooth, meaningful functioning of daily life is not the ultimate goal, but merely a prerequisite for achieving maximum personal freedom and independence. the standardization of practical life processes, as sought by the bauhaus, therefore does not mean a new enslavement and mechanization of the individual, but rather frees life from unnecessary ballast, thus allowing it to unfold all the more freely and richly.

in order to satisfy these aspirations, "the greatest effect must be achieved with the least means." our technology-driven times have rapidly become aware of this old precept when solving material questions; it dominates the work of technicians. the economy of the intellect asserts itself more slowly, for it requires more knowledge and cultivation of thought than economy in the material sense. here is the focal point between civilization and culture! it sheds light on the essential difference between the product of technology and economy, the sober work of the calculating mind as opposed to the "work of art," the product of passion. that is the objective sum of the labor of countless individuals; this, moreover, is also a unique result, a self-contained subjective microcosm whose universal validity grows with its creator's maturity.

what attracts the artistic designer to the perfection of technology? t h e  m e a n s  o f  h i s  d e s i g n ! because his inner truth, the concise, unfussy, functionally appropriate execution of all his parts to form an organism, the bold use of new materials and methods is also a logical prerequisite for artistic creation.

the "work of art" must "function" in the spiritual as well as in the material sense, just like the product of the engineer, e.g. an airplane whose natural purpose is to fly. in this sense, the artistic creator can see his model in the technical product and receive inspiration for his own work from the deepening of his process of creation without leaving his own field, whose essence differs from the technical process of creation. because the work of art is always a product of technology

---

●) see bauhausbücher vol. 7: walter gropius, "principles of bauhaus production."

too, yet at the same time must still fulfill spiritual purposes, which can only be made apparent by means of imagination and passion.

and this is where the bauhaus is confronted with another major problem: what is space? what means are used to design it? ●) the problem-posers among the modern painters were the ones who began to reconquer abstract space; that is why they were indispensable in constructing the new bauhaus doctrine. spatial relationships were explored and developed in pictorial composition, in the home, in devices and on the stage, while objectively ascertainable elements were incorporated into the teaching.

the first productive results of the bauhaus's pioneering work, shown in its exhibition in weimar in 1923 under the motto "art and technology a new unity," established the reputation of the much-contested institute in the eyes of the public. its ideas became the leaven that drove development and clarification of problems everywhere.

despite this, it faced serious crises. threatened by an uncomprehending and hostile government, the director and the masters' council decided in 1924 — in order to prevent the institute's destruction — to publicly declare the dissolution of the bauhaus at their own initiative, aware of their solidarity and the strength of their moral rights as its creators. despite all predictions to the contrary ●●) this step proved to be the right one. in terms of human ties, the intellectual front that had formed, linking the leading masters who had gradually been called to the bauhaus — lyonel feininger, wassily kandinsky, paul klee, gerhard marcks, ladislaus moholy-nagy, georg muche, oskar schlemmer ●●●) — and the students withstood this test. the students, too, on their own initiative, declared to the government their solidarity with the director and the masters and declared they were leaving the school. this united stance of the bauhaus was echoed throughout the press and decided its fate. various cities — dessau, frankfurt a. m., hagen i. w., mannheim, darmstadt — began talks to take on the bauhaus. dessau, at the heart of the central german lignite mining district, with its booming economy, decided — guided by its farsighted mayor hesse — to take in the bauhaus in its entirety. when the contracts in weimar expired, the masters and students moved to dessau in spring 1925 and began rebuilding the bauhaus. thuringia was forced

●) see the introductory chapter "space" in moholy-nagy's "from material to architecture" (bauhausbücher vol. 14).

●●) by way of explanation. the following criticism by an expert in "baugilde" illustrates the animosity to which the bauhaus was opposed: "actually, no one murdered the bauhaus! it killed itself! ... do we still have to build schools in germany today that cultivate the ability to create interesting superfluous objects for well-to-do classes? do we have to train young people to fill the dreariness and emptiness of our so-called cultural circles with ever new art confectionery that turns the stomachs of those who make it?" h. de fries.

●●●) j. itten and l. schreyer had resigned in previous years.

to abandon its legal claims to the name "bauhaus" and the government of anhalt confirmed the new institute as the "bauhaus dessau, hochschule für gestaltung." the city administration took a consistent approach when it took in the bauhaus; it approved a new building for the institute with a special residential building for the students and seven apartments in semidetached houses for the masters based on my proposals and entrusted me with constructing these buildings, which at the same time generated welcome practical activity for the workshops.

the basis of the bauhaus's work, especially its teaching, was carefully revised at the same time after the experiences of the weimar years, after six bauhaus students, josef albers, herbert bayer, marcel breuer, hinnerk scheper, joost schmidt and gunta stölzl were appointed to teaching posts and to the masters' council. the students' representatives participated actively in the overall organization. the ideas and plans developed in weimar were consolidated and gradually realized, and their social impact became apparent. ties to industry became more closely knit and the workshops gained certain preparatory experimental laboratories for serial production of industrial products. teaching of construction was expanded by involving specialized teachers, and the foundation course and design teaching, the vital artery of the common bauhaus work, received new, lively impetuses.

in the meantime, after a one-year construction phase, it was possible to move into the new bauhaus building, which was inaugurated in december 1926 with a new exhibition attended by numerous guests from germany and abroad.

the uniform appearance of the results of its work — as manifested in this book — despite the diversity of the individuals working together, was the fruit of the jointly developed bauhaus spirit. the "bauhausbücher," the "bauhaus" journal and the lectures at the bauhaus evenings, which had already been held during the weimar period, kept the complex of questions raised by the bauhaus vital and in motion, warding off the risk of academic stultification at an early stage. but at the same time, the struggle against imitators and misunderstandings had to begin, against those who wanted to see a "bauhaus style" in all buildings and devices of the modern age that lacked decoration and threatened to homogenize the well-substantiated meaning of the bauhaus's work. the goal of the bauhaus is not a "style," not a system, dogma or canon, not a recipe or a fashion! it will remain alive as long as it does not cling to the form, but seeks the fluid essence of life itself, underlying the changeable form!

the bauhaus was the first institute in the world to dare to enshrine this anti-academic attitude in a school. in order to ensure its ideas would be victorious, it took on the duty of leadership, maintaining the vigilant vitality of its comrades-in-arms, the sole manner to ensure reciprocal interpenetration of imagination and reality. but a "bauhaus style" would mean regressing to academic stagnation, to the life-threatening inertia that the bauhaus was once created to combat. may the bauhaus be preserved from this death!

when i left the bauhaus in spring 1928 after nine years of struggle and responsibility to return to my own building activities, the ideas of the bauhaus had gained a foothold among the general public. the first and most difficult part of its task had been fulfilled.

●

with the illustrations and remarks in this book, i wish to give an account of my own work as an architect and building project organizer during my dessau bauhaus years. this work was a product of the atmosphere that was created during the years of bauhaus construction and offered a foretaste — with all the necessary consequences of the struggle — of its new technical and formal results.

the means of depicting buildings in a book are very limited. photography cannot reproduce the experience of space. the true proportions of a room or a building in relation to our fixed, absolute body size create intriguing tensions in the viewer in front of the building itself, which the reduced scale of an image cannot convey at all. after all, mass and space are also receptacles and backdrops for life itself, which they are supposed to serve — the processes of movement that take place within them can only be represented in a figurative sense. for all these reasons, i believed that the essence of these buildings, the order of the life functions taking place in them and the resulting spatial expression could only be reproduced by leading the reader past numerous photos of details one after the other, in order to convey the illusion of the spatial sequence envisaged through these changing views.

the city of dessau had entrusted me with the overall direction — planning, contracting-out of work and construction project management — for all the buildings, so that all the individual work was carried out by me at the bauhaus and could be uniformly integrated. all the designs and construction plans were created in my private studio; ●) nevertheless, i publish the buildings under the name "bauhaus buildings." because the public rightly saw in them the fruit of the constant intellectual exchange that prevailed at the bauhaus and the masters and workshops had, moreover, independently planned and executed major aspects of the fittings. ●●)

---

●) the following architects worked in my architectural office on planning and execution of the buildings: karl fieger, friedrich hirz, max krajewski, fritz levedag, otto meyer-ottens, ernst neufert, heinz nösselt, richard paulick, herbert schipke, bernhard sturzkopf, franz throll, walter tralau, hans volger.

●●) the bauhaus carpentry workshop supplied furniture and fittings, the metal workshop provided light fixtures, the weaving workshop upholstery and curtain fabrics, the mural painting department was responsible for the buildings' external and internal colour design and the print shop contributed the lettering.

**bauhaus building dessau**
**built in 1926**
**architect: walter gropius**

**the bauhaus building,**

commissioned by the city of dessau, was begun in autumn 1925, completed after one year of construction and inaugurated in december 1926.

the whole building covers about 2 630 sqm of land and has a cubic volume of c. 32 450 cbm. it cost 902 500 mk or 27.8 mk per cbm including all additional costs. the fixtures cost 126 200 mk.

**the entire architectural ensemble consists of three parts:**

**1 the "technische lehranstalten" wing**

(subsequently the vocational college) contains administrative offices and classrooms, a staff room, library, physics laboratory, model rooms, fully developed lower ground floor, a mezzanine floor and two upper floors. on the first and second upper floors, a bridge on four columns, with the bauhaus administrative offices on the lower level and the architecture department on the upper level, spans the road and leads to the building containing the

**2 laboratory workshops and classrooms of the bauhaus.**

on the lower ground floor, the stage workshop, print shop, dye works, sculpture, packing and storage rooms, caretaker's apartment and boiler room with a coal cellar in front of it.

on the mezzanine floor, the carpentry workshop and the exhibition rooms, a large vestibule, adjoining it the auditorium with the raised stage in front of it.

on the first floor: the weaving workshop, the rooms for the foundation course, a large lecture theatre and the connection between building **1** and building **2** through the bridge.

on the second floor: the mural painting workshop, metal workshop and two lecture theaters, which can be combined to form a large exhibition hall. followed by the second level of the bridge where the architecture department has its offices along with the architectural studio baubüro gropius.

the auditorium in the ground floor of this building leads via a single-story intermediate building to the

**3 studio building,** which contains the recreational facilities for the students; both sides of the stage between auditorium and dining room can be opened during performances, allowing the audience to sit on both sides. for festive occasions, all stage walls can be opened, so that the sequence of dining room, stage, auditorium, vestibule can be combined to form one large space for festivities.

the dining room is adjoined by the kitchen with its ancillary rooms. outside the dining room is a spacious terrace, which is adjoined by a large sports ground.

the five upper floors of the studio building contain 28 residential studios for bauhaus students, with a kitchenette on each floor. all four floors of the studio building and the roof terrace are connected to the kitchen by a dumbwaiter.

the lower ground floor of the studio building contains bathrooms, a gymnasium with changing rooms for sportspeople and a laundry with electrical equipment.

**material and construction of the entire ensemble:**

reinforced concrete skeleton with brick masonry. reinforced slabs on structural supports, in the lower ground floor "mushroom-construction ceiling." all windows have steel window sashes with double weathering contacts with polished plate glass. the roof terraces with welded asphalt tiles on a torfoleum insulation layer, the non-accessible flat roofs are covered with lacquered burlap over a torfoleum insulated layer and levelling concrete. drainage is through cast-iron pipes inside the building with no use of zinc sheeting. exterior finish cement plaster with keim mineral paint.

the colorful design of the interiors throughout the entire building was executed by the bauhaus mural painting department. design and execution of all the lighting fixtures came from the bauhaus metal workshop. the tubular steel furniture for the auditorium, dining room and studios was produced to designs by m. breuer. the lettering was executed by the bauhaus printing department.

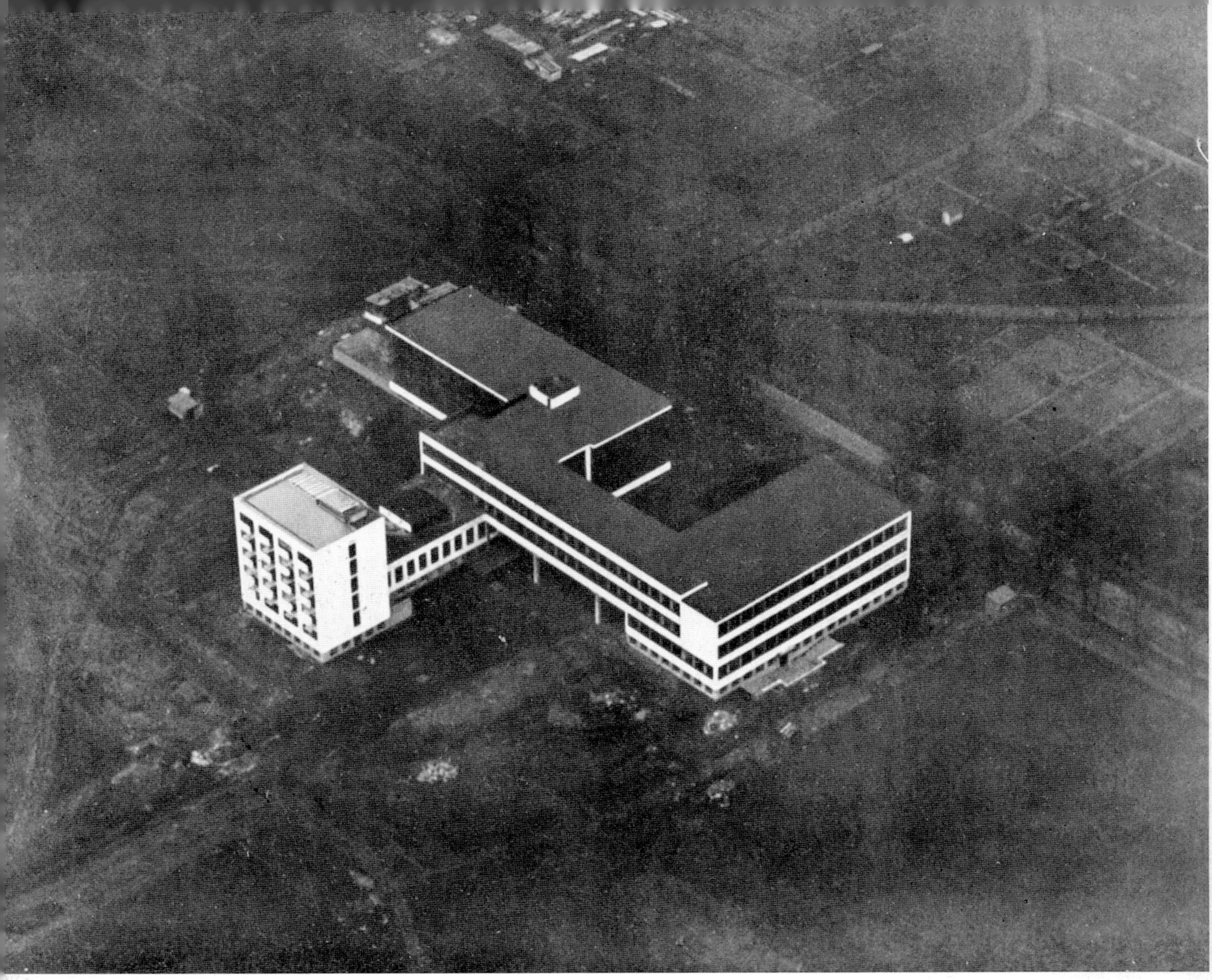

**fig. 1** **bauhaus building**
bird's-eye view

aerial photo r. petschow / berlin

air transport routes pose a new challenge to builders of houses and cities:
to consciously design the buildings' appearance from a bird's-eye view too, which in the past was not visible.

**fig. 2** **bauhaus building**
bird's-eye view

aerial photo r. petschow / berlin

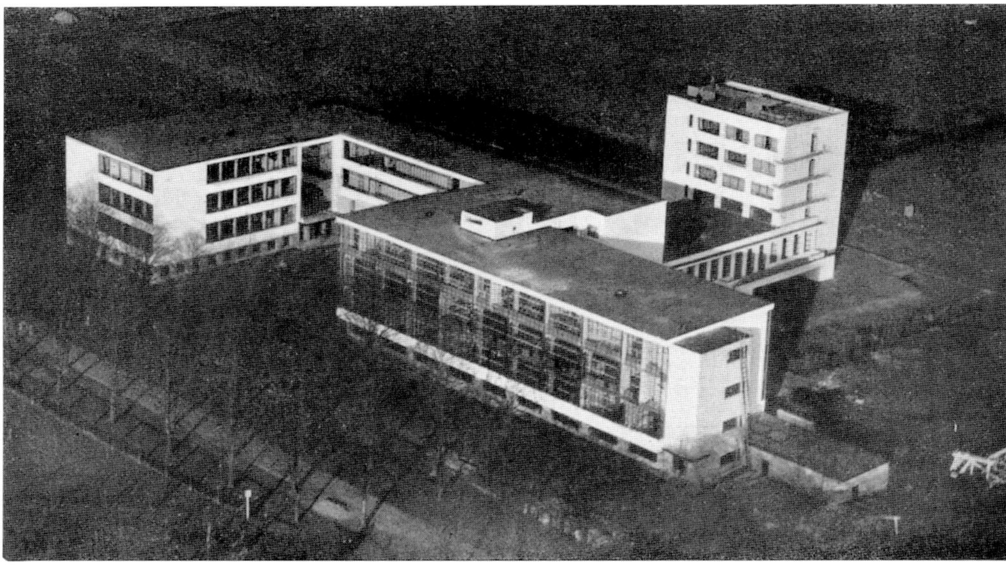

junkers-luftbild / dessau

**fig. 3** **bauhaus building**
bird's-eye view

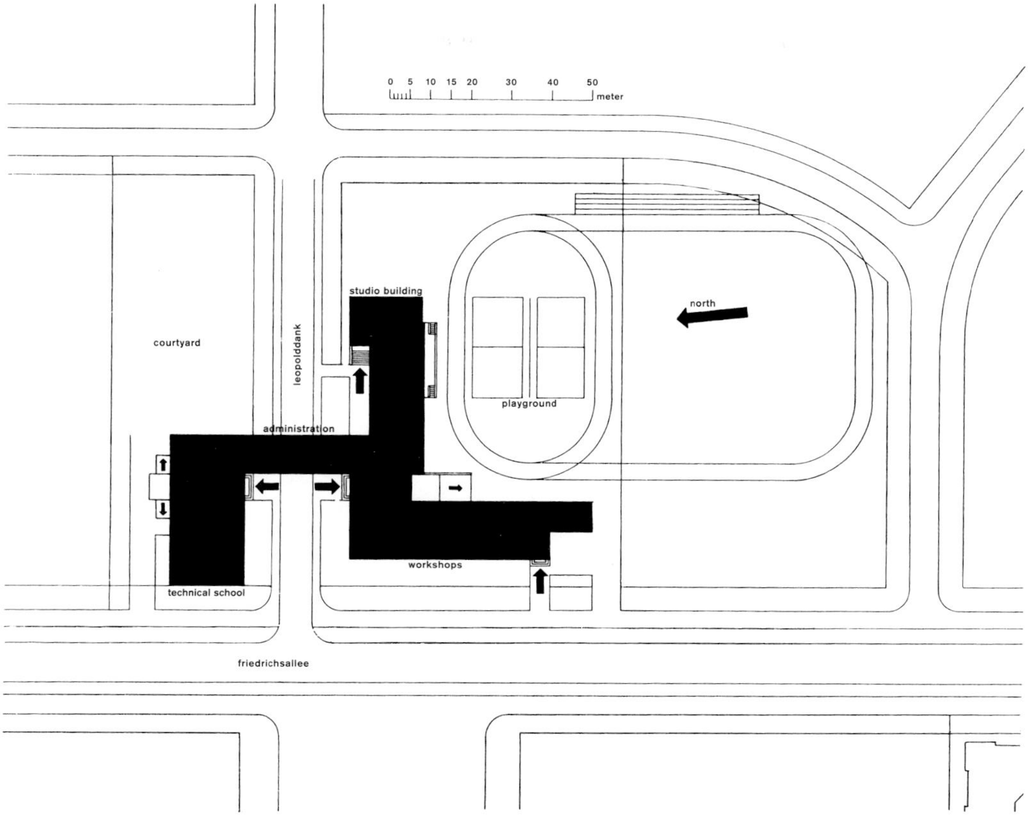


**fig. 4** **bauhaus building**
site plan of the entire ensemble

a typical renaissance or baroque building has a symmetrical facade with a central axis leading up to the entrance. approaching, the viewer sees a two-dimensional image.

a building born of the spirit of our times moves away from the imposing manifestation of the symmetrical facade. you have to walk right around this building to grasp its physicality and the function of its parts.

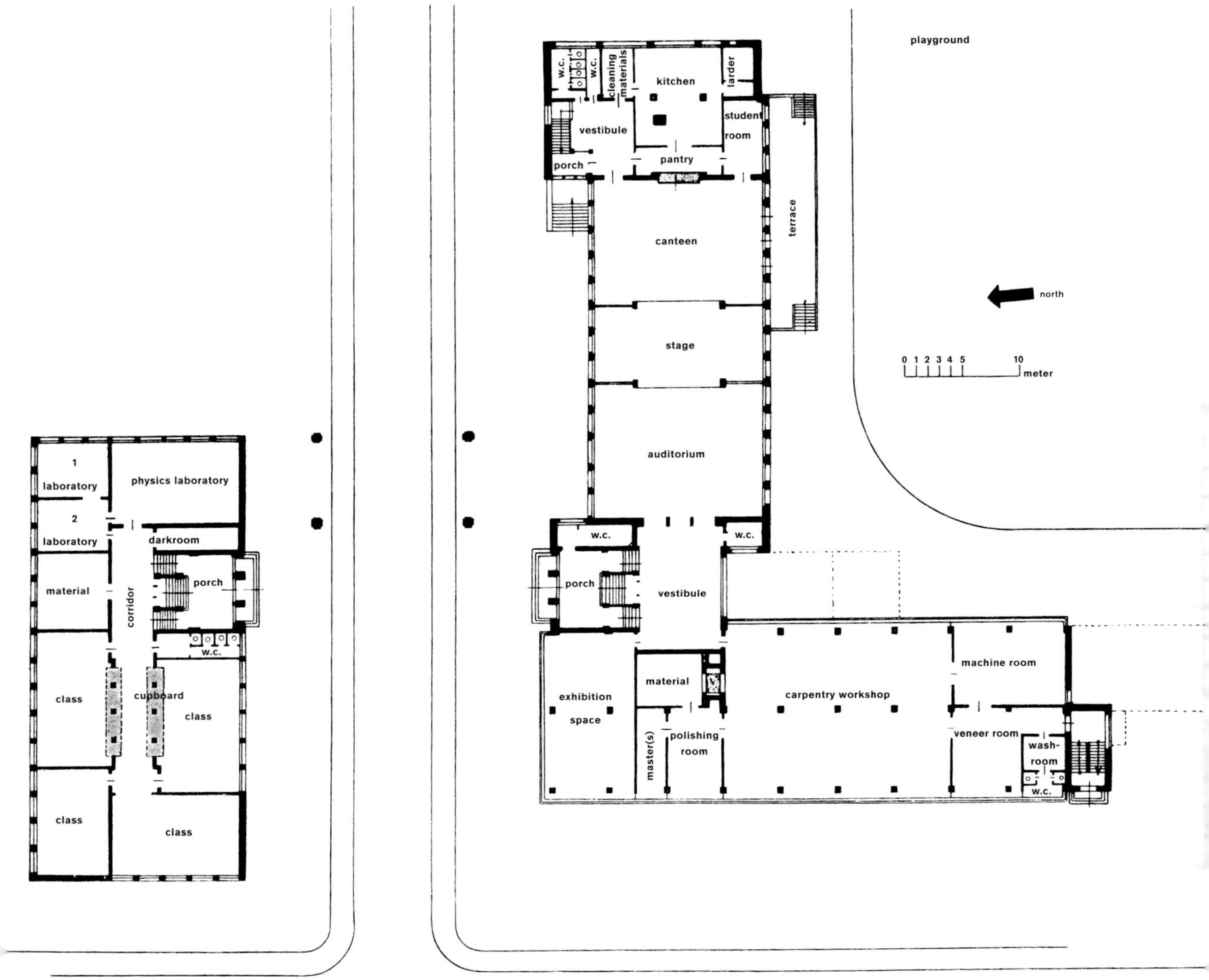


**fig. 5** bauhaus building
floor plan of ground floor

goal for the organization of a good floor plan:
correct use of incident sunlight,
short time-saving routes,
clear separation of the organism's various divisions
possibility of varying the sequences of rooms to respond to any organizational changes that may become necessary by means of ingenious axial division.

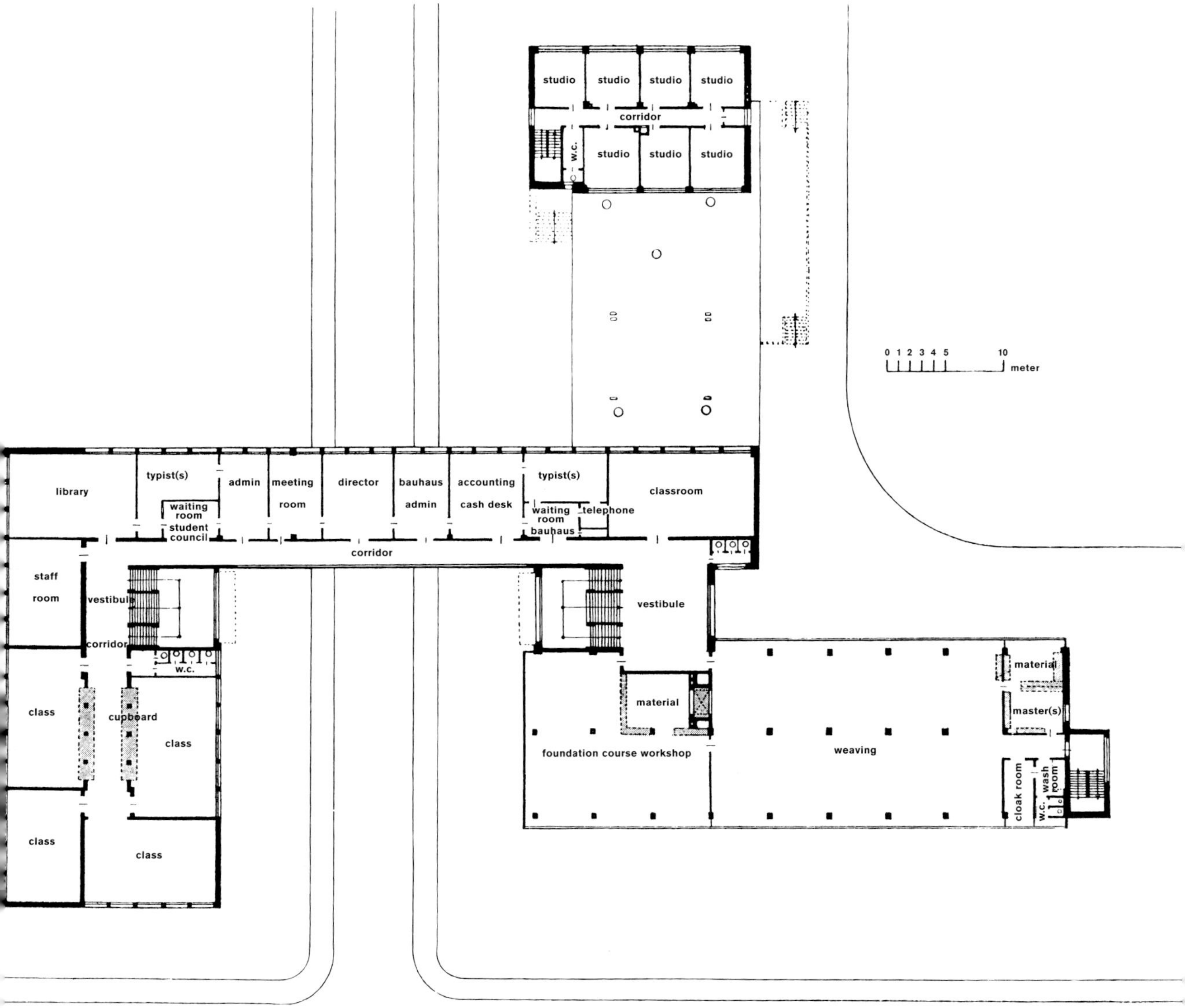


**fig. 6** bauhaus building
floor plan of the 1st floor

**fig. 7** bauhaus building as a skeleton construction 1926
east view

photo wedekind / dessau

photo lucia moholy / berlin

**fig. 8** **bauhaus building as a skeleton construction 1926**
southeast view

## material and construction methods:

tamped concrete foundations.
supporting framework made of reinforced concrete pillars with reinforced brick ceilings set between them and partial masonry infill.
the workshop building has no masonry on its side walls, the internal pillars fulfill the function of a load-bearing outer wall.
the cantilevered ceilings bear the weight of the iron-framed network of windows that close off the rooms. in the basement a "mushroom-construction ceiling" without beams to reduce construction height.
the roof terraces on the studio building are covered with welded asphalt panels on a heat-insulating torfoleum underlay, the other flat roofs, which are not accessible, are covered with cold-cut varnish (awegit) on jute fabric over torfoleum underlay and an additional concrete layer.
drainage is provided throughout by cast-iron pipes that descend inside the buildings, making external zinc drainpipes unnecessary.
the exterior finish on the masonry consists of water-repellent smooth cement plaster with a coat of white keim mineral paint.

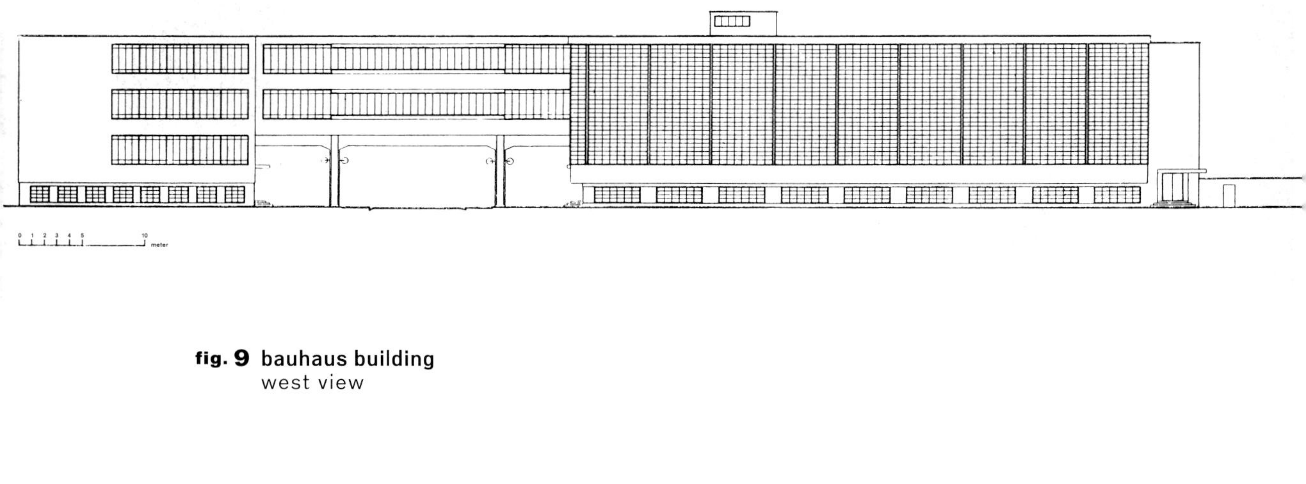


**fig. 9** bauhaus building
west view

**fig. 10** **bauhaus building**
northwest view

photo lucia moholy / berlin

the outside wall of the workshop building has a completely transparent appearance with sash bars and glazing. the load-bearing pillars are located inside, behind the glass wall. (see figs. 32 and 43)
the bridge-like structure along the street is the result of constructing two separate school institutions with separate entrances (on the left the "technische lehranstalten," on the right the actual "bauhaus"). the shared administrative offices are located on the bridge and can be accessed from the interior on both sides.

**fig. 11** **bauhaus building**
east view with section through the auditorium

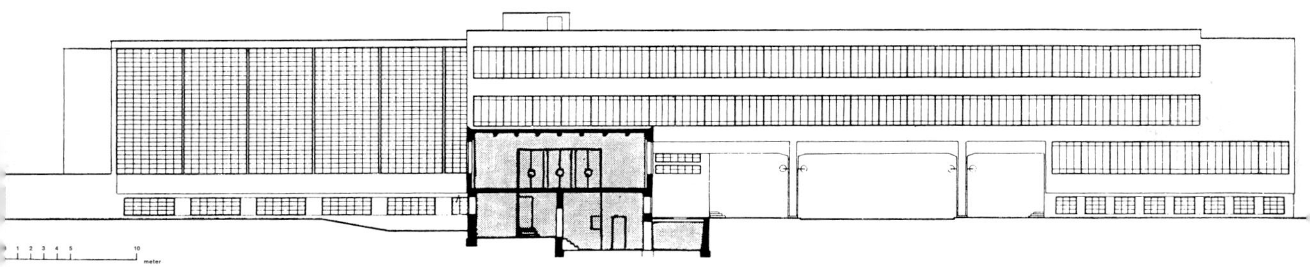

**fig. 12** **bauhaus building**
northeast view

the load-bearing pillars (see fig. 7) are located behind the metal framing elements of the strip windows, made of steel profiles with glazing.

photo lucia moholy / berlin

left in the picture, at a distance from the school building, the accommodation block with 28 studios for students; in the low intermediate building, dining room, kitchen, bathroom and gym, stage and lecture theater.

photo lucia moholy / berlin

**fig. 14** **bauhaus building**
bridge construction between the main building and the “technische lehranstalten” wing on the day of the inauguration; on the right white, yellow, red and blue flags
first floor: administrative offices
second floor: architecture department

photo photothek / berlin

← **fig. 13** **bauhaus building**
connecting passage between the first floor and the bridge

the supporting bridge piers (see fig. 14) under the inner wall (right in the photo), the corridor landing is cantilevered. steel-frame windows with glazing.

**fig. 15** bauhaus building
east-west section (see fig. 16)

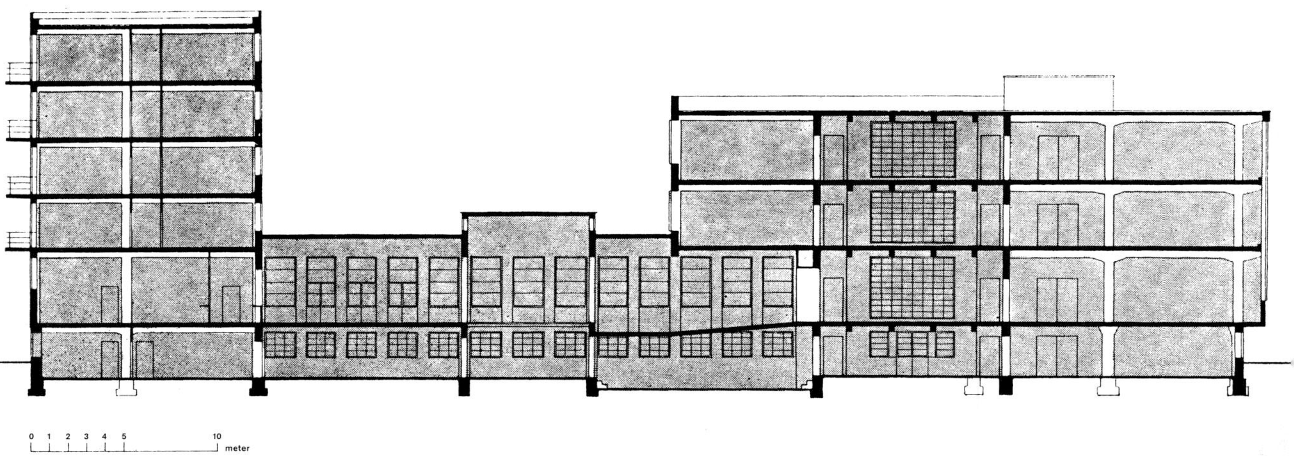

photo photothek / berlin

**fig. 16** **bauhaus building**
north view toward studio building, dining room with stage

**fig. 17** **bauhaus building** from the "ufa" film of the inauguration (december 1926)
northwest view toward the bridge

**fig. 18** bauhaus building
southeast view

from the "ufa" film of the inauguration (december 1926)

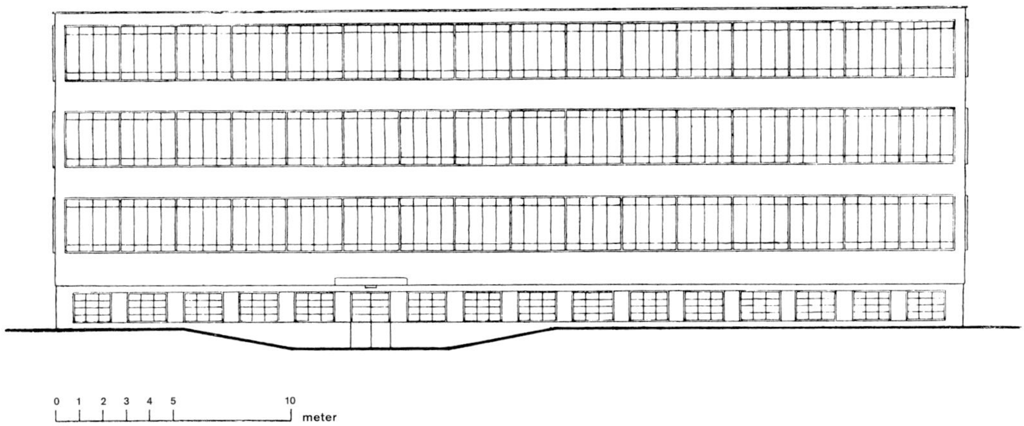


**fig. 19** **bauhaus building**
north view of the "technische lehranstalten" (see fig. 20)

the load-bearing concrete pillars of the skeleton are positioned behind the joints of the projecting strip window, that is, above the visible intermediate columns of the cellar windows (see also fig. 20).

the iron-framed windows with upper and lower ventilation flaps ensure favorable air inflow and outflow for the classrooms, a type of window that has been used repeatedly in germany ever since. glazing in polished plate glass.

**fig. 20** **bauhaus building** photo lucia moholy / berlin
northwest view of the “technische lehranstalten”

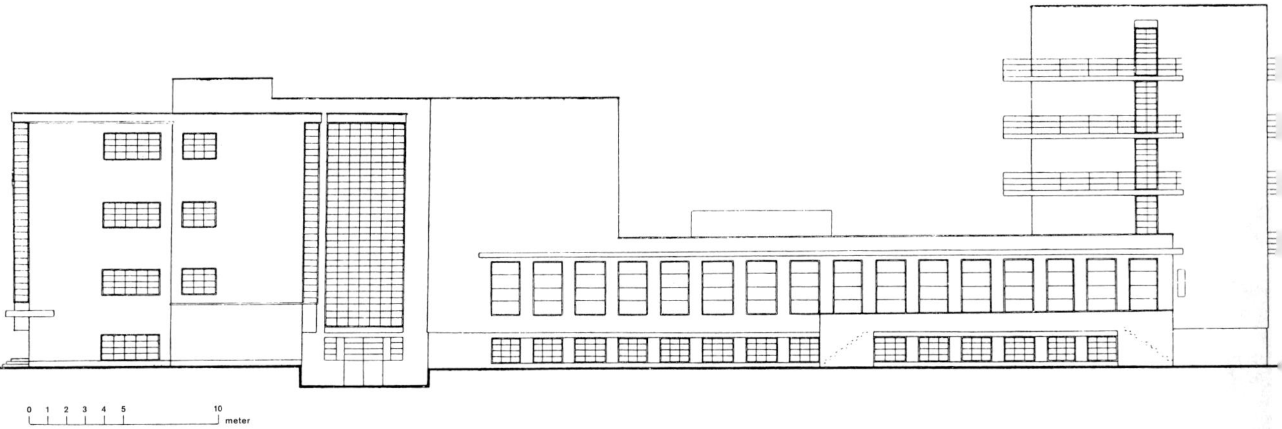


**fig. 21** **bauhaus building**
south view (see fig. 22)

as a result of planned rationalization methods, technical development in the building industry is today more than ever under the influence of the old precept: *achieve the greatest effect with the least means.* the rapid development of technical means promotes the technicians' goal of making architectonic structures more open, i.e. saving on mass, space, weight and site traffic.

**fig. 22** **bauhaus building**
south view

photo hertig / bauhaus

in the world of design, new, industrially processed construction materials are competing with old natural construction materials and are beginning to overtake them. the strength and molecular density of these new construction materials — iron, concrete, glass — have made it possible to construct spaces and buildings with wide spans that are flooded with light, making the greatest possible savings in construction mass, projects for which the building materials and technology of the past were insufficient. these space-saving constructions in iron and concrete, which are becoming more and more daring, with the deliberate aim of increasingly diminishing the spatial dimensions of the building's load-bearing structure by means of sophisticated calculations and the utmost quality improvements in material strength, consistently lead to ever larger wall and roof openings, which allow daylight to flow unhindered into the rooms while protecting the interior from the weather. old-style house walls with small openings set within large, unbroken areas and uninterrupted roofs give way to the converse principle of extensive window areas and roof openings within narrow frames of structural beams and columns that are as pared down as possible.

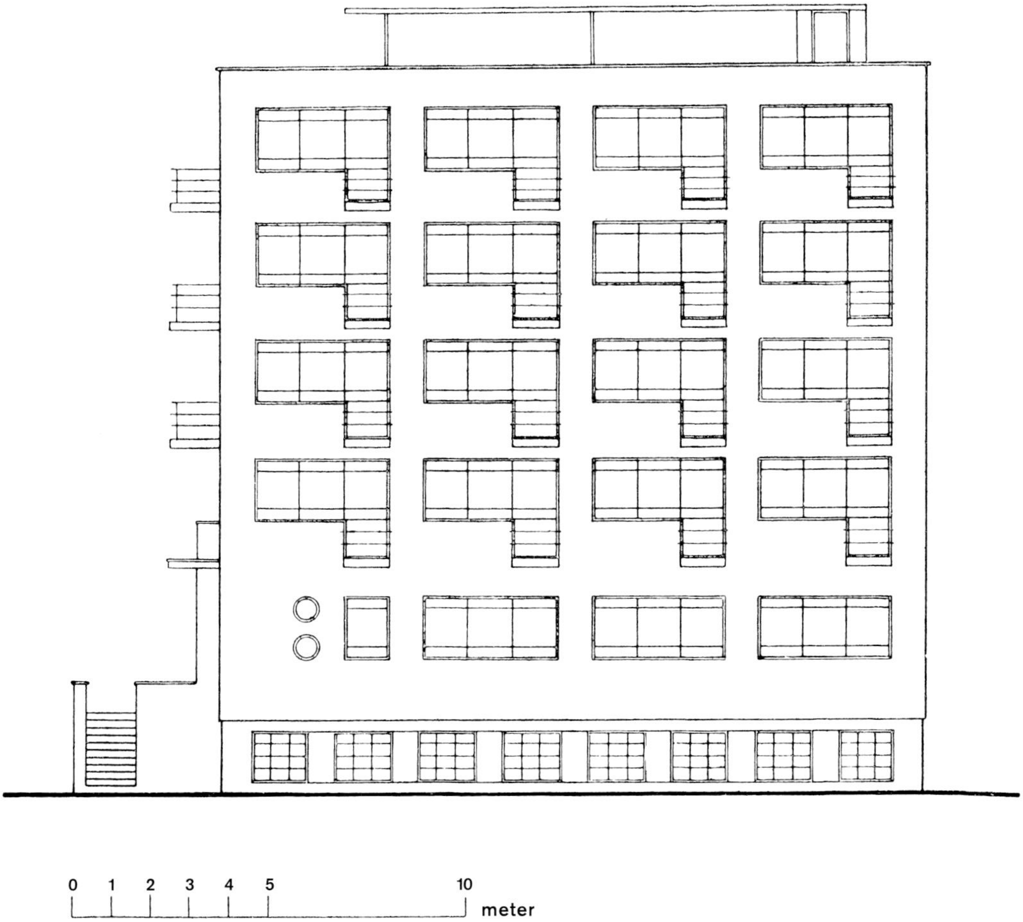


**fig. 23** bauhaus building
east view of the studio building

photo wedekind / dessau

**fig. 24** bauhaus building
east view

the idea that people who work on a communal task, as in the bauhaus, must have an opportunity to retreat from the community and withdraw completely into themselves for a while without being disturbed, meant that the building containing the students' studios has been moved away from the rest of the activities and each individual studio has been afforded as much peace and quiet as possible, even giving each studio its own little balcony.

**fig. 25** bauhaus building
south side of the studio building by night

photo lyonel feininger / dessau

**fig. 26 bauhaus building**
southeast view of the studio building

each student studio consists of a 5.17/4.35 m (center-to-center distance) room, with an alcove for the bed, washstand with running water and two built-in cupboards. shared kitchenettes on each floor. dumbwaiter. (see figs. 59 and 60)

photo consemüller / bauhaus

photo lyonel feininger / dessau

**fig. 27** bauhaus building
balconies of the studio building by night

**fig. 28** bauhaus building
individual balconies in the studio building
photo wutke / moscow

**fig. 29** bauhaus building
entrance to the main building and transverse glass facade of the workshop building

photo lucia moholy / berlin

photo lucia moholy / berlin

**fig. 30** **bauhaus building**
view from bridge structure toward studio building, dining room and stage

**fig. 31** **bauhaus building**
northwest view

photo lucia moholy / berlin

**fig. 32** **bauhaus building** photo lucia moholy / berlin
northwest corner of the workshop building, on the left, entrance to the "technische lehranstalten"

at the corner of the workshop building the structural framework of the concrete pillars and massive ceilings can be clearly identified. for the first time the problem of rendering the wall more transparent was followed through to its logical conclusion by extending a continuous glass skin in front of the supporting structural skeleton. the cantilevering of the ceilings above the basement brings twofold advantages: structurally beneficial and therefore economical shortening of distances from the outer pillars to the central pillars in the interior and the option of using the entire glazed facade in front of the pillars for workplaces in the workshops too.
low radiators across the whole width of the glass wall. curtains for the windows are hung from the ceilings along the whole glass wall to protect against the sun's rays.

**fig. 33** bauhaus building
main entrance

**fig. 34** **bauhaus building**
partial view of the workshop building
photo lux feininger / bauhaus

as a modern construction material, glass will play an essential role in the development of modern construction methods especially due to increasingly large openings. its application will be unlimited and not confined to windows; because its noble properties, its transparent clarity, its light, floating, immaterial materiality guarantee modern architects' love.

**fig. 35** **bauhaus building**
side entrance to the main staircase from the courtyard. on the left workshop building, on the right auditorium

photo lucia moholy / berlin

photo lucia moholy / berlin

**fig. 36** bauhaus building
view onto the workshop building from the main staircase window with single plate glass pane

**fig. 37** **bauhaus building**
corner of the main staircase and the workshop building

photo itting / bauhaus

photo atlantik / berlin

**fig. 38** bauhaus building
view from the landing of the main staircase in the "technische lehranstalten" building. ventilation is by means of interconnected pivoting windows that can be held open at any angle.

photo lucia moholy / berlin

**fig. 39** bauhaus building
roof garden on the studio building (the students' gymnasium). the surrounding parapet is designed as a bench. floor covering made of welded asphalt panels.

successful experience over the last 20 years with the construction of flat roofs, both as roof terraces and nonaccessible versions, have convinced me that technically advanced people will use only the horizontal roof in future. because its advantages over the old sloping roof are so numerous, it is only a matter of time until the final victory of the flat roof. the use of accessible roof gardens filled with plants is an effective means of integrating nature into the stony desert of the big city. with gardens on terraces and roofs, the cities of the future will create an impression (seen from the air) of being one large garden. the cultivatable land lost through construction of the houses will be regained on the flat roofs.

the other advantages of flat roofs are: unencumbered rectangular attic spaces instead of the difficult to exploit blind spots under pitched roofs; avoidance of wooden roof trusses, which are a frequent cause of roof fires; scope to use the roof area for purposes related to residence (children's playgrounds, drying clothes); improved scope for extension and construction on all freestanding sides of the cubic structure; no wind-exposed area, therefore less need for repair (roof tiles, slate, shingles); avoidance of connections, gutters and drainpipes made of perishable zinc sheet.

**fig. 40** **bauhaus building**
view onto the terrace outside the dining room

photo bayer

photos:
figs. 41, 42, 44, 45, 47 lux feininger / bauhaus
figs. 43, 46 bayer / berlin

**figs. 41—47** bauhaus building
life at the bauhaus

since the weimar bauhaus era, a tradition of "bauhaus festivities" had developed: with the welcome challenge of executing the improvised ideas of masters and students, festive rooms, costumes, performances. these festivities were one of the most powerful means of creating friendship and cohesion in the bauhaus and were an unforgettable experience for everyone who took part.

**fig. 48** bauhaus building
northeast view by night, bauhaus festivities for the building's inauguration with several thousand guests from germany and abroad

**fig. 49** **bauhaus building**
northwest view by night. the nighttime illumination allows the structural framework of the building to be seen particularly clearly

**fig. 50** bauhaus building
iron-framed window of a workshop room. pillar behind the outer glass skin, therefore narrower pillar and cantilevered ceilings. radiators along the glass wall. interlinked pivot window sections

bauhausfoto

**fig. 51 bauhaus building**
window of the bathing area on the basement floor

**fig. 52 bauhaus building**
iron-framed window of the auditorium and the dining room. the wheel on the lower right simultaneously operates three to four windows, each with four interconnected pivot sections

photos consemüller / bauhaus

photo consemüller / bauhaus

**fig. 53** **bauhaus building**
hallway and staircase of the "technische lehranstalten" (see floor plan fig. 6)

economic solution for a school corridor enclosed on two sides. illumination of the longitudinal corridor walls by double-glazed sound-insulated skylights above the drawing-board cupboards. cross ventilation through the classrooms opposite and through the windows in the staircase.

**fig. 54** **bauhaus building**
main staircase
steps and top of balustrade with white and black terrazzo tiles

photo consemüller / bauhaus

photo consemüller / bauhaus

**fig. 55** **bauhaus building**
entrance vestibule with the three doors to the auditorium
light fixtures and color design:
moholy-nagy with the bauhaus workshops

**fig. 56 bauhaus building** photo consemüller / bauhaus
auditorium
tubular steel chairs: marcel breuer
lighting: bauhaus metal workshop (moholy-nagy)
color design: bauhaus mural painting department (scheper)

the auditorium with adjoining stage, whose rear wall can also be opened onto the dining room, is used for meetings, lectures and performances. diffuse, non-dazzling lighting with tubular lamps. in the top right of the image, slit for film and projection equipment.

**fig. 57 bauhaus building**
teachers' room of the "technische lehranstalt" with cupboards for the teachers and cabinets for storing drawings
color design: bauhaus mural painting department (scheper)

photo consemüller / bauhaus

photo consemüller / bauhaus

**fig. 58** bauhaus building
the director's study. this is where the joint meetings of the masters' council and the students' representatives were held
color design: bauhaus mural painting department (scheper)

photo consemüller / bauhaus

healthy, well-lit workplaces boost performance!

**fig. 59 bauhaus building**
weaving workshop looms and winding machine. roof drainage on the inner pillars.
unplastered whitewashed ceilings
healthy, well-lit workplaces boost performance!

**fig. 61** **bauhaus building**
metal workshop, spinning lathe and grinding machine

bauhausfotos

**fig. 60** **bauhaus building**
metal workshop, drilling machine

**fig. 62** **bauhaus building**
metal workshop, workplaces

photo m. brandt / bauhaus

photo m. brandt / bauhaus

the current division between training young people in craftsmanship on the one hand and industry on the other is illogical and outdated. the old manual apprenticeship needs instead to be supplemented by a technical apprenticeship that teaches every apprentice the basics of and interrelationships between modern industrial working methods.

**fig. 63** bauhaus building
metal workshop, in the foreground lathe lining and parts for light fixtures

bauhausfotos

**fig. 64** **bauhaus building**
carpentry workshop

bauhausfotos

**fig. 65** **bauhaus building**
mural painting workshop. on the wall systematic experiments with various painting techniques on a plaster ground

**fig. 66** **bauhaus building**
preliminary course practical work and drawing hall

photo peterhans / bauhaus

photo peterhans / bauhaus

**fig. 67 bauhaus building**
drawing hall

drafting room of the architecture department, on the left side partition wall to the hallway made up of cabinets for drawings and construction material samples. homogenous lighting of the workplaces by continuous window strip.

**fig. 68** **bauhaus building**
food serving in the dining room, the pivot windows in the iron-framed windows are visible in the background

bauhausfoto

photo consemüller / bauhaus

a person who builds must, over and above technical abilities, be familiar with the particular design questions that relate to space. the means of addressing them arise from the natural physiological facts of the human genus; they take precedence above the secondary demands of the race, the nation, the individual.

**fig. 69 bauhaus building**
dining room
in the background white and black folding doors to stage
furniture: bauhaus carpentry workshop (m. breuer)
light fixtures: bauhaus metal workshop (moholy-nagy)
color design: bauhaus mural painting department (h. scheper)

**fig. 70** bauhaus building
kitchenette in the studio building on each floor, one per 7 studios, shared balcony outside it

photo peterhans / bauhaus

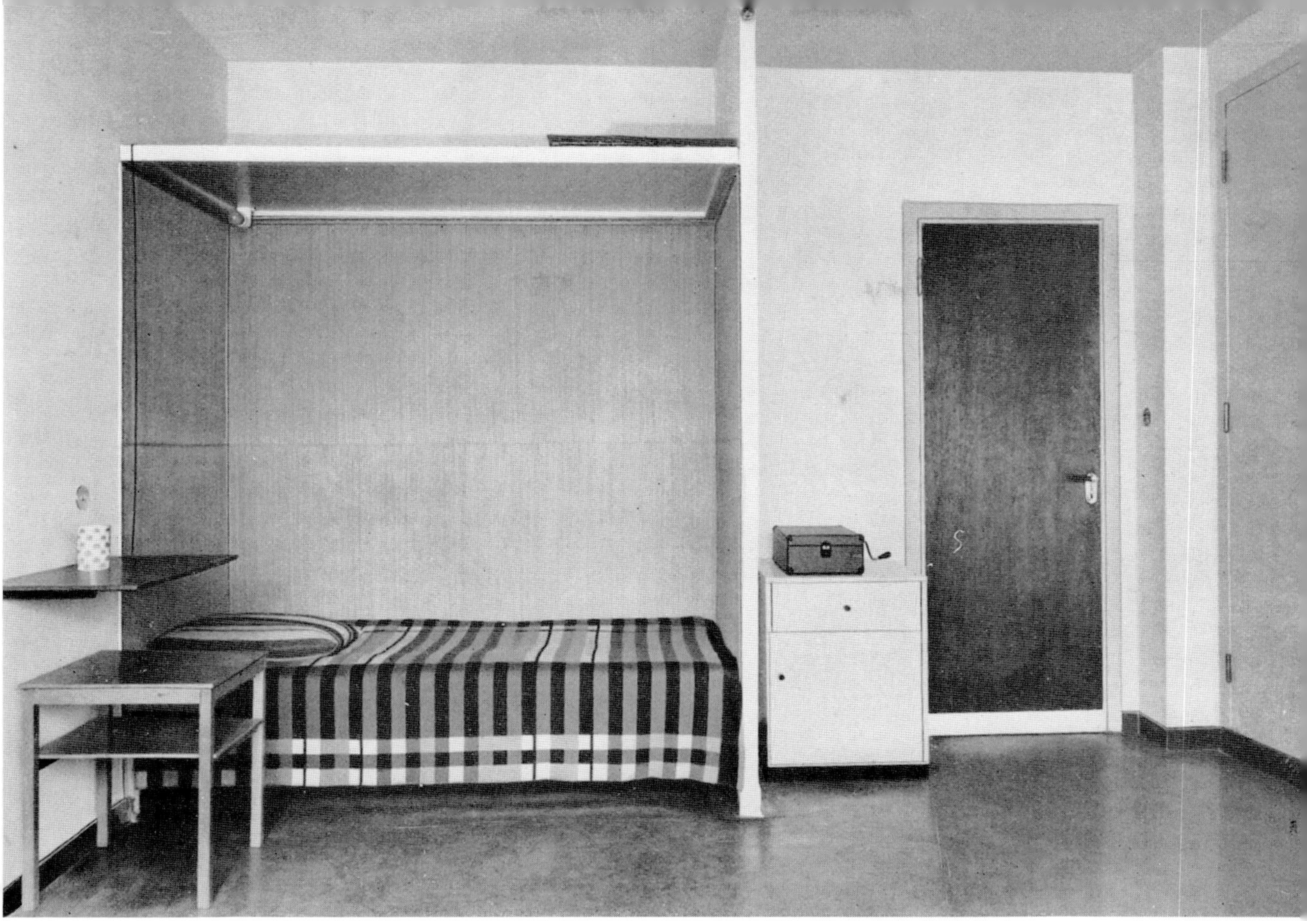

photo peterhans / bauhaus

**fig. 71** bauhaus building
student studio in the studio building with bed in alcove, 2 built-in cupboards, washstand with hot-and-cold running water, desk and chair

**fig. 72** bauhaus building
washroom in the workshop building

photo consemüller / bauhaus

**fig. 73** **bauhaus building**
telephone, rotatable, between two workshop rooms

photo consemüller / bauhaus

**fig. 74** **bauhaus building**
light fixtures of the classrooms:
bauhaus metal workshop

photo lucia moholy / berlin

the bead of the glass dome for semi-indirect lighting is the result of the technical glassmaking method of precision joints welding the opal glass (below) to the matt glass (above). "making a virtue out of the seam" (schinkel).

aerial view r. petschow / berlin

**fig. 75** **bauhaus building**
bird's-eye view

for obvious reasons, the general public is primarily interested in the external appearance of buildings. humankind's natural inertia prevented public opinion from adapting rapidly to the changed new forms. the history of technology shows that new technical inventions are initially concealed behind the mantle of the past that they adopt by way of imitation. the first automobiles looked similar to the stagecoach! but gradually, as a result of the rapid development of technology, people today have become accustomed to accepting new, logically developed outward appearances. hand in hand with technology, modern architecture has developed a characteristic countenance that differs significantly from that of the old craftsmanship in construction. its typical hallmarks are its clear, well-proportioned features, free of all unnecessary ingredients, also inherent in modern engineering products, unburdened by an old world of ideas that had different technical requirements. the creative architect is primarily interested in discovering new functions and mastering them technically and creatively. the decisive factor in assessing a building remains determining whether the architect and engineer have, with the least possible expenditure of time and material, created an instrument that functions, i.e. that perfectly serves the required purpose in life, which can be derived from both psychological and material requirements.

**bauhaus masters' apartments**
**built in dessau 1925/1926**
**architect: walter gropius**

**the bauhaus masters' apartments,**

commissioned by the city of dessau, were started in the summer of 1925 and were available for use after one year of construction. the detached house has a volume of 1908 cbm, the three semidetached houses each have 2507 cbm. the detached house cost 61860 rm, or 32.4 rm per cbm, the semidetached houses cost 81500 rm, or 32.5 rm per cbm including all additional costs.

**the four buildings** —

a detached house and three semidetached houses — are surrounded by low-density pine woodland and positioned 20 m apart in an east-west facing row on a smooth lawn with unfenced grounds. the row of houses is flanked by a garage and garden wall adjacent to the detached house by the roadway.

**construction materials:**

tamped concrete foundations. walls: jurko blocks made of slag, sand and cement in medium-sized slabs that can be moved by one man. reinforced concrete lintels. reinforced-brick ceilings partly cantilevered to form terraces. all windows glazed in polished plate glass. individual central heating in each house unit. flat roofs not accessible: tar and gravel roof; accessible roof surfaces: artificial stone panels over a tar and gravel roof.

**the detached house:**

basement with three-room apartment for the estate janitor (garden and heating maintenance), heating and storage cellar. the ground floor is the residential level, combined living and dining room, two bedrooms, kitchen, bathroom. the upper floor contains only a guest room, maid's room, laundry and ironing room with electrical equipment and a box room. in all rooms cupboards and shelves are built-in, set within the wall or forming the wall. stipulation of clear housekeeping procedures, avoidance of idling and restlessness. the roof-garden terraces and garden are incorporated into the organism for living in.

**the semidetached houses:**

all six apartments in the three semidetached houses are the same down to the last detail and yet different in their effect. simplification through multiplication means reduction in price and accelerated construction. the floor plan of one of the two apartments in each house is the interlinked mirror image of the floor plan of the other, rotated through 90 degrees from east to south. exactly the same components are used, but the appearance of each half is different due to their interlacing. the difference in height between the studio and the residential rooms reinforces this impression. the studio, staircase, kitchen, pantry and bathroom face north, away from direct sunlight; the living room, dining room, bedroom and children's room with the garden, terraces, balconies and roof gardens face toward the sun. the utility rooms, the living room and dining room are on the ground floor, the bedrooms and studios on the upper floor.

the color design executed by the bauhaus mural painting department emphasizes the spatial organization within the apartments, but at the same time creates pronounced variations in the effect of rooms that are otherwise identical.
furniture: bauhaus carpentry workshop (m. breuer), light fixtures: bauhaus metal workshop (moholy-nagy).

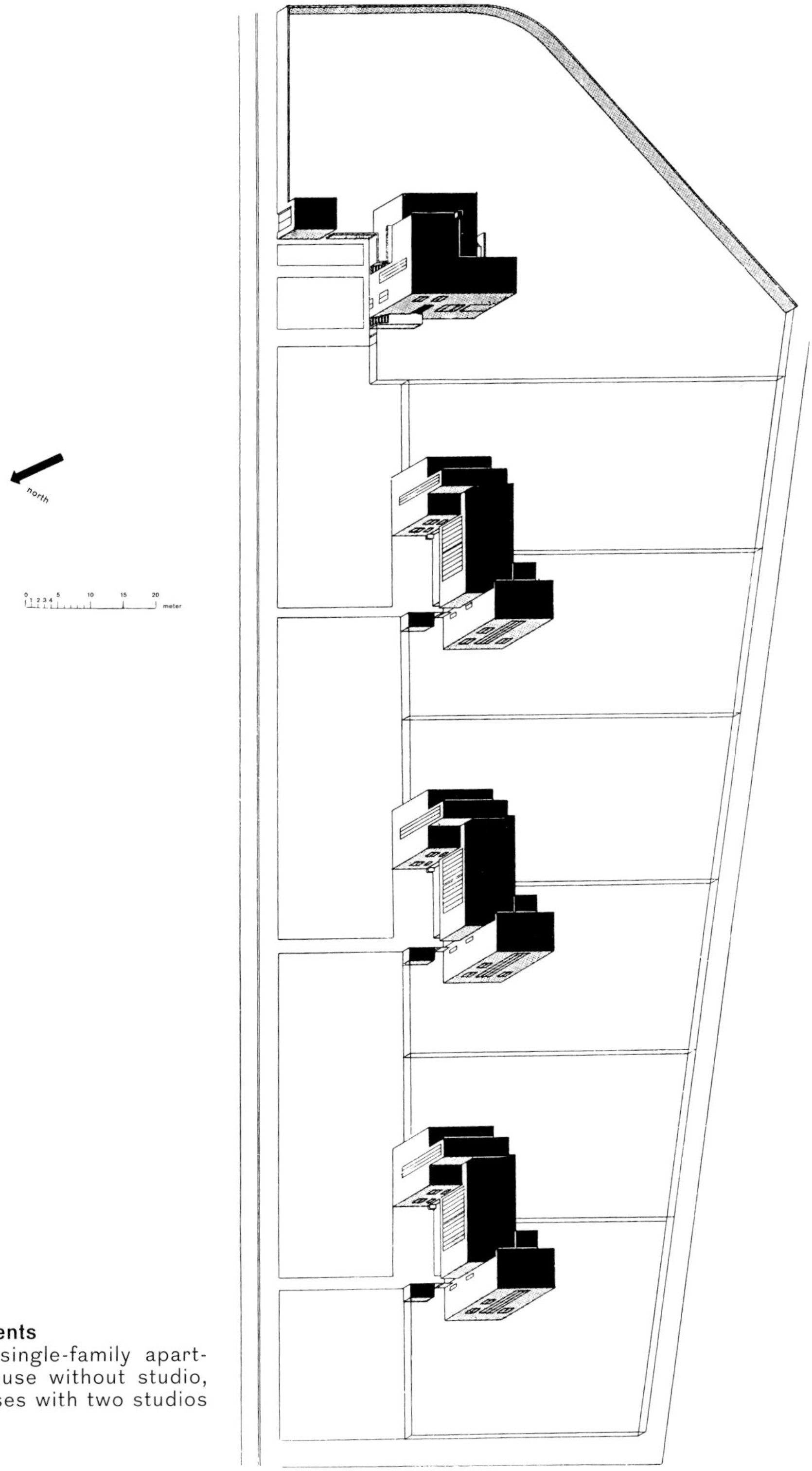


**fig. 76** **bauhaus masters' apartments**
site plan of the seven single-family apartments; one detached house without studio, three semidetached houses with two studios each

photo lucia moholy / berlin

**fig. 77** **bauhaus masters' apartments**
street (northwest) view of a semidetached house

the intermingling of trees and vegetation growing between the buildings, which opens up and closes off the view, ensures pleasant contrasts, renders the schematic structure more supple and enlivens it, mediates between the buildings and people and creates a sense of tension and scale.
for architecture is not solely about fulfilling a purpose, unless we consider that our psychological needs for harmonious space, for the consonance and proportion of the elements that enable us to perceive the vitality of the space, are actually higher-order purposes.

**fig. 78** **bauhaus masters' apartments**
garden (east) view of gropius's detached house

photo lucia moholy / berlin

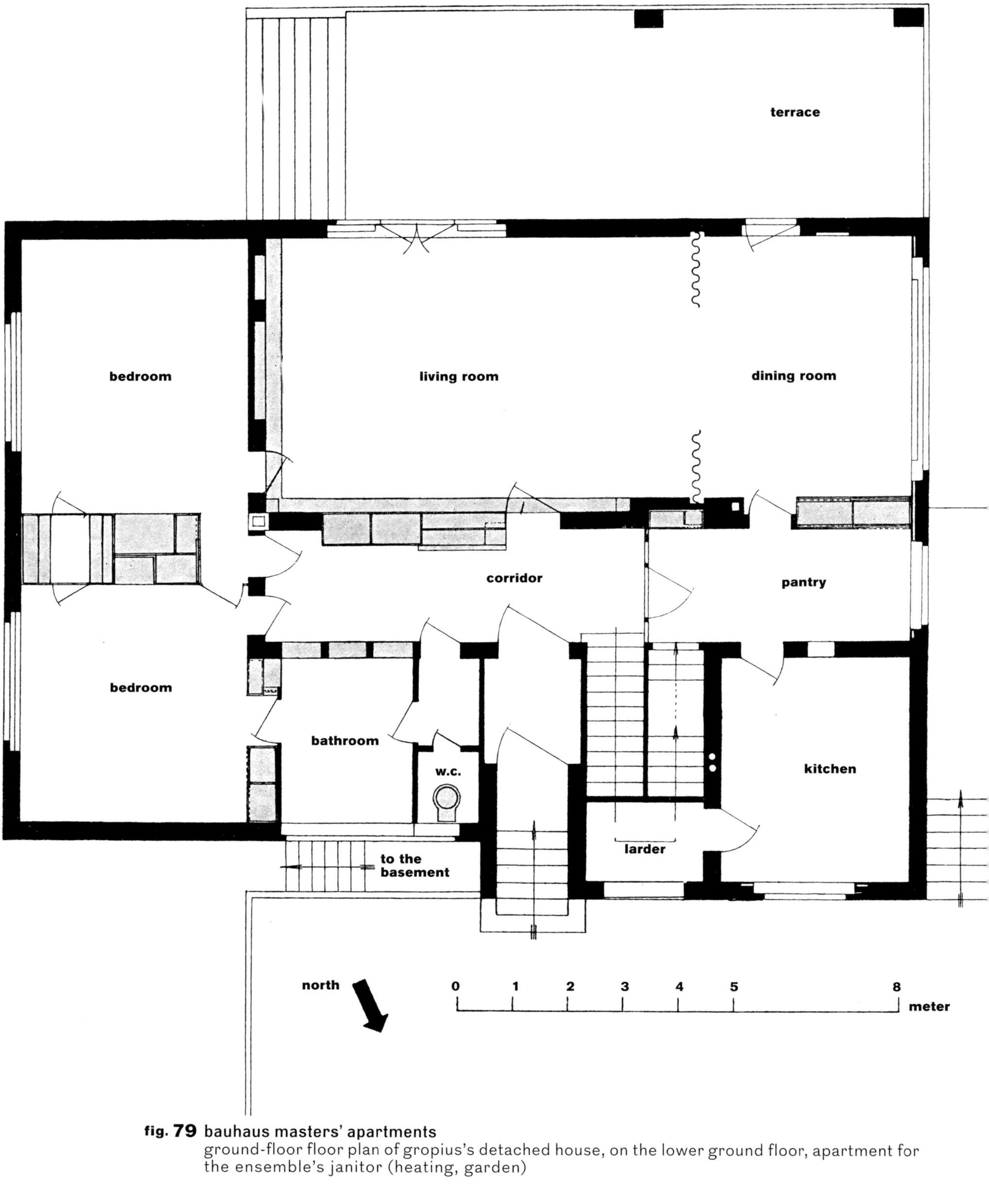


**fig. 79** bauhaus masters' apartments
ground-floor floor plan of gropius's detached house, on the lower ground floor, apartment for the ensemble's janitor (heating, garden)

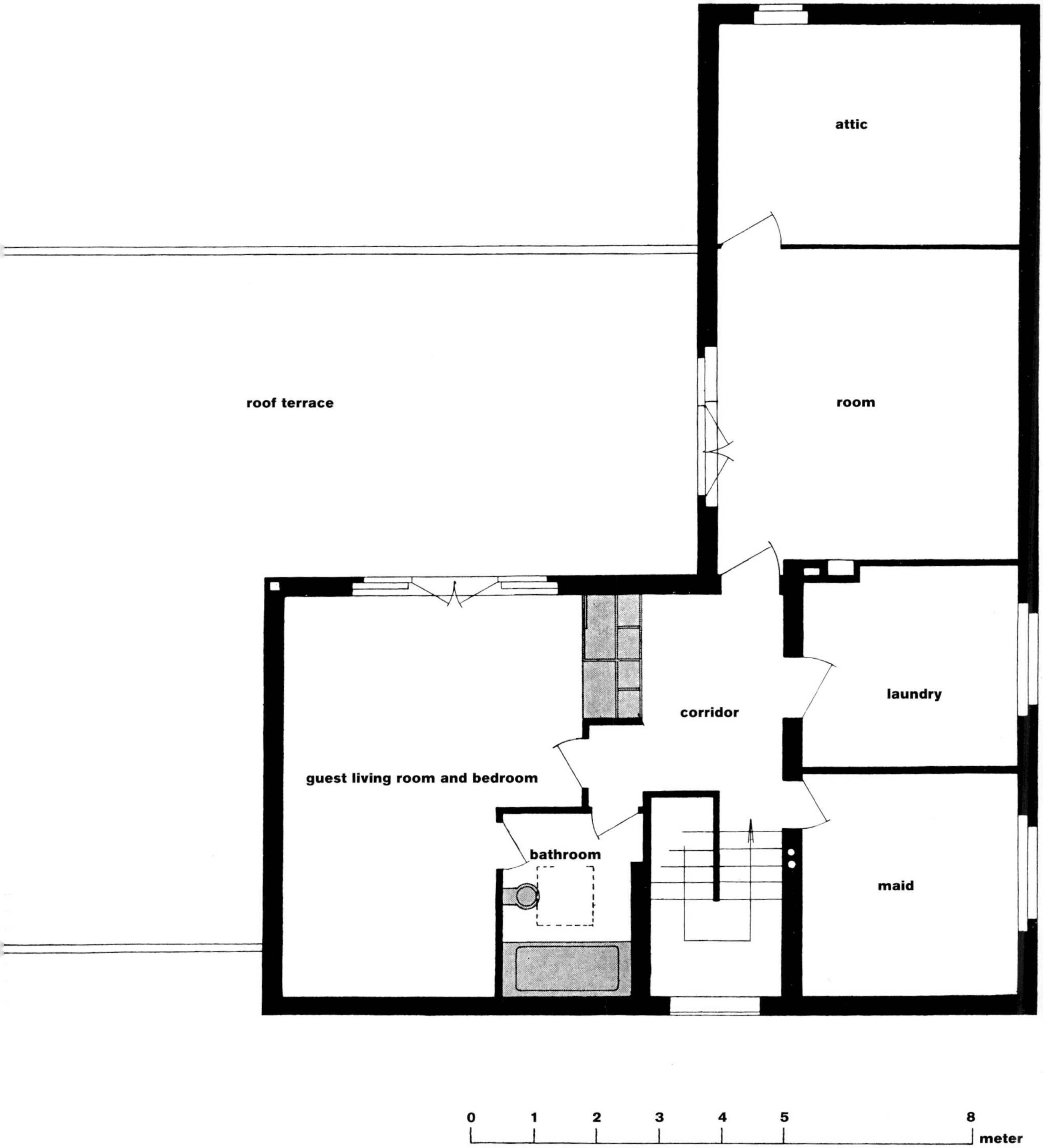




**fig. 80** bauhaus masters' apartments
upstairs floor plan of gropius's detached house

building means designing life processes. the organism of a house results from the sequence of processes that unfold within it. in a residential dwelling, the functions of living, sleeping, bathing, cooking, eating inevitably give shape to the entire structure of the house. the processes are different in railway stations, factories, churches, but true form stems solely from these processes. the form of the building is not there for its own sake, it arises solely from the nature of the building, from the function that it is intended to fulfill.

**fig. 81 bauhaus masters' apartments**
street (north) view of gropius's detached house
with main entrance

photo lucia moholy / berlin

photo ise gropius

**fig. 82** bauhaus masters' apartments
west view of gropius's detached house with side entrance

**fig. 83** **bauhaus masters' apartments**
northeast view of gropius's detached house with garage (on the right)

photo lucia moholy / berlin

photo lucia moholy / berlin

**fig. 84** bauhaus masters' apartments
west view of gropius's detached house with side entrance

**fig. 85** **bauhaus masters' apartments**
south view of gropius's detached house with lower and upper terrace

photo ise gropius

photo ise gropius

**fig. 86** **bauhaus masters' apartments**
southeast view of gropius's detached house with view of a pair of semidetached houses on the ground floor, covered terrace outside the dining room and steps to the garden. on the upper floor area for sunbathing and taking the air with orange curtains

**fig. 87** bauhaus masters' apartments
vestibule by the main entrance to gropius's detached house

photo lucia moholy / berlin

humboldt-film / berlin

**fig. 88** bauhaus masters' apartments
built-in cloakroom fittings in the vestibule of gropius's detached house

the natural scale of the human body, its natural movements and functions are decisive in determining the proportions and heights of the various pieces of furniture. our life today is different from that of our ancestors, our social and family circumstances have changed. the position of contemporary women in working life, less settled lifestyles and more cramped living conditions give rise to certain demands that clamor to be satisfied. we have no time to imitate, out of false sentimentality, bygone social forms and lifestyles, created for completely different conditions. our grandparents needed different furniture than we do in the age of cars and trains. we do not exist for the sake of furniture, as it often seems today, but vice versa.

**fig. 89 bauhaus masters' apartments**
combined living and dining room in gropius's detached house
lighting fixture: bauhaus metal workshop
color design: m. breuer and bauhaus murals workshop
furniture: marcel breuer

photo lucia moholy / berlin

photo lucia moholy / berlin

smooth, meaningful functioning of daily life is not an end in itself, but merely the prerequisite for achieving the maximum degree of personal freedom and independence. the standardization of practical life processes therefore does not signify a new enslavement and mechanization of the individual, but instead liberates life from unnecessary ballast, so that it can unfold all the more fully and free of shackles.

**fig. 90** bauhaus masters' apartments
dining room in gropius's detached house with cupboard and hatch to sink
sun protection: roller blind
color design: m. breuer and bauhaus mural painting department
built-in cupboard: w. gropius and m. breuer

**fig. 91** **bauhaus masters' apartments**
dining room in gropius's detached house with crockery cupboard
color design: m. breuer and mural painting department
steel furniture: marcel breuer
reducing the load-bearing walls to pillars offers scope to use the wall space for built-in cupboards

photo agfa / berlin

humboldt-film / berlin

**fig. 92** bauhaus masters' apartments
boswik grid in front of the large dining-room window in gropius's detached house

photo stone / berlin

**fig. 93** **bauhaus masters' apartments**
double desk in the living room of gropius's detached house (marcel breuer)

**fig. 94** bauhaus masters' apartments
vertical filing system in the double desk in gropius's detached house

a clearly arranged domestic archive enables the housewife to find her bearings quickly when managing household matters.

humboldt-film / berlin

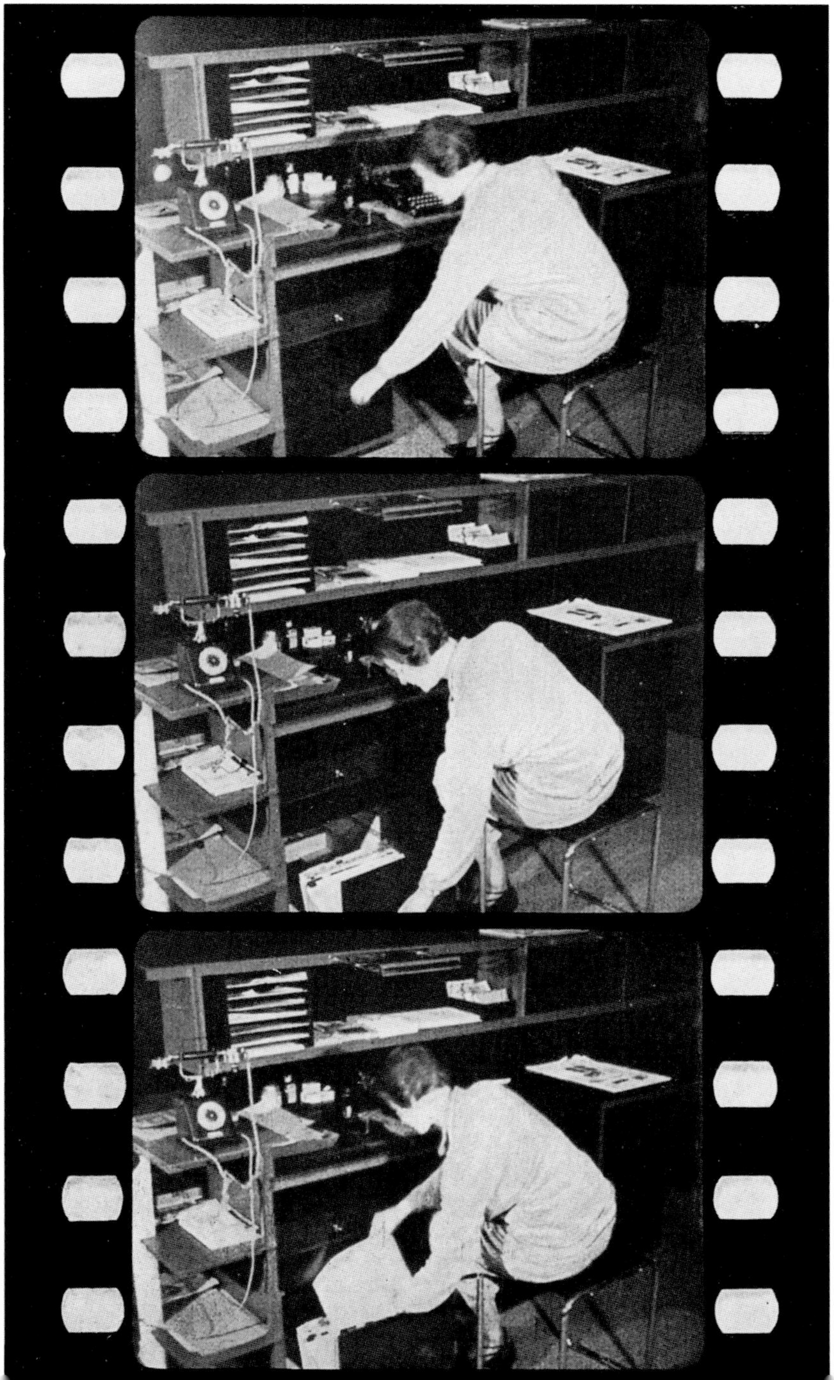

photo lucia moholy / berlin

**fig. 95** bauhaus masters' apartments
folding desk lamp at the double desk of gropius's detached house (bauhaus metal workshop, m. brandt)

photo lucia moholy / berlin

**fig. 96** bauhaus masters' apartments

picture alcove with adjustable frame for paintings or drawings, prints or photos. below: cutlery cabinet with fold-out serving table, dining room of detached house.

photo lucia moholy / berlin

**fig. 97** **bauhaus masters' apartments**
tea-making corner in the living room of gropius's detached house
inlet and outlet for hot and cold water
power outlets for electrical devices

photo lucia moholy / berlin

**fig. 98** bauhaus masters' apartments
sewing cabinet and bookshelves (marcel breuer) in the living room of gropius's detached house

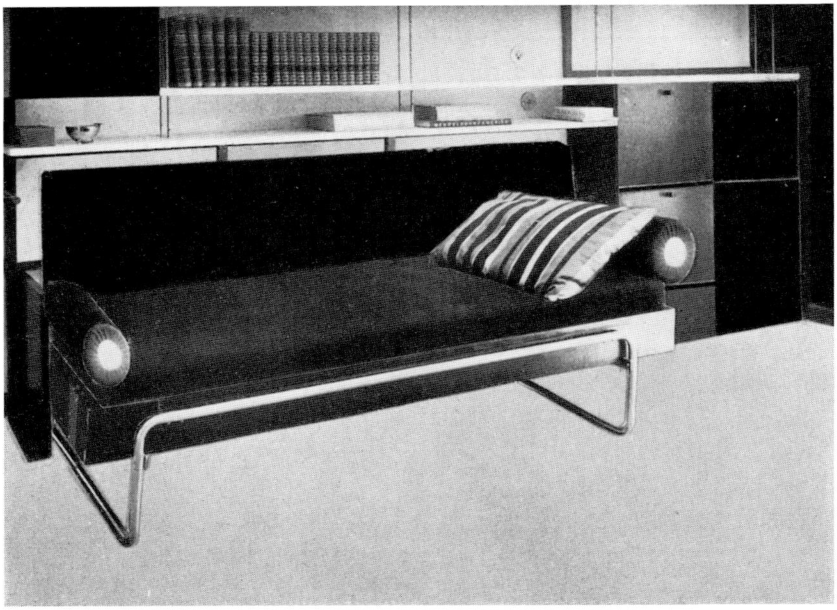

photo lucia moholy / berlin

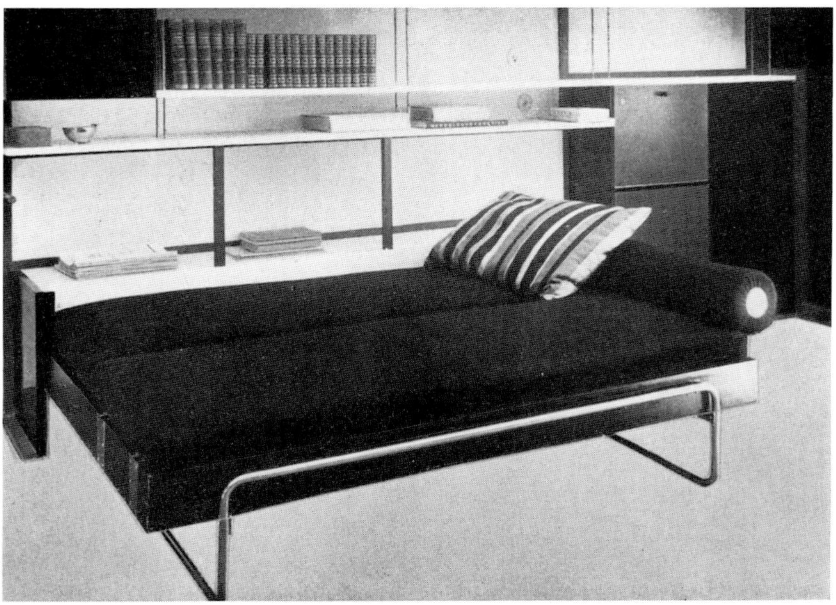

**figs. 99/100** bauhaus masters' apartments
pull-out double sofa (w. gropius and m. breuer) in the living room of gropius's detached house

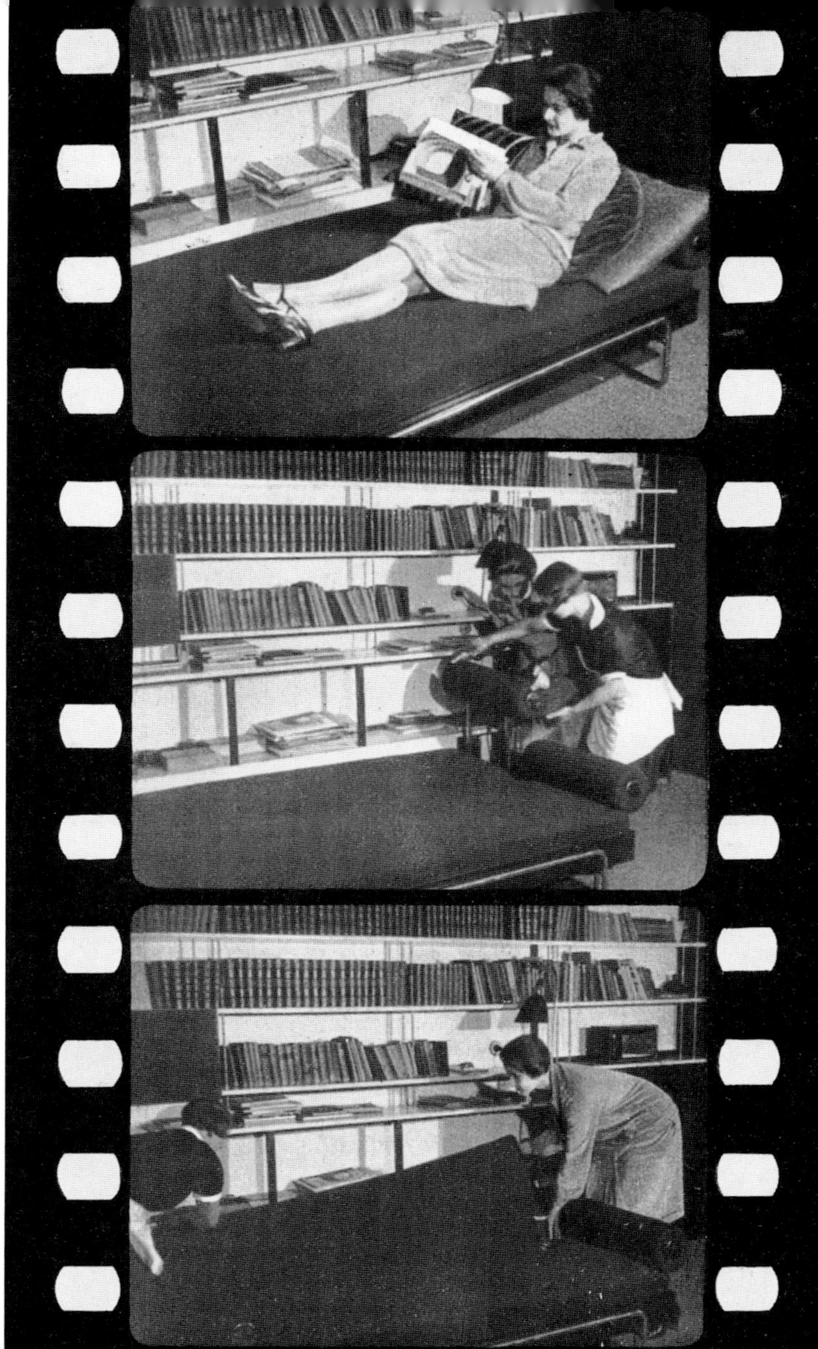

humboldt-film / berlin

**fig. 101** bauhaus masters' apartments
pull-out double sofa (w. gropius and m. breuer) in the living room of gropius's detached house

photo lucia moholy / berlin

today, many things still seem luxurious,
which will very soon become the norm!

**fig. 102** **bauhaus masters' apartments**
fan in the living room of gropius's detached house (junkers-werke)
a heating unit connected to the central heating is installed in the wall behind the fan, allowing the fresh air drawn into the room to be heated in winter

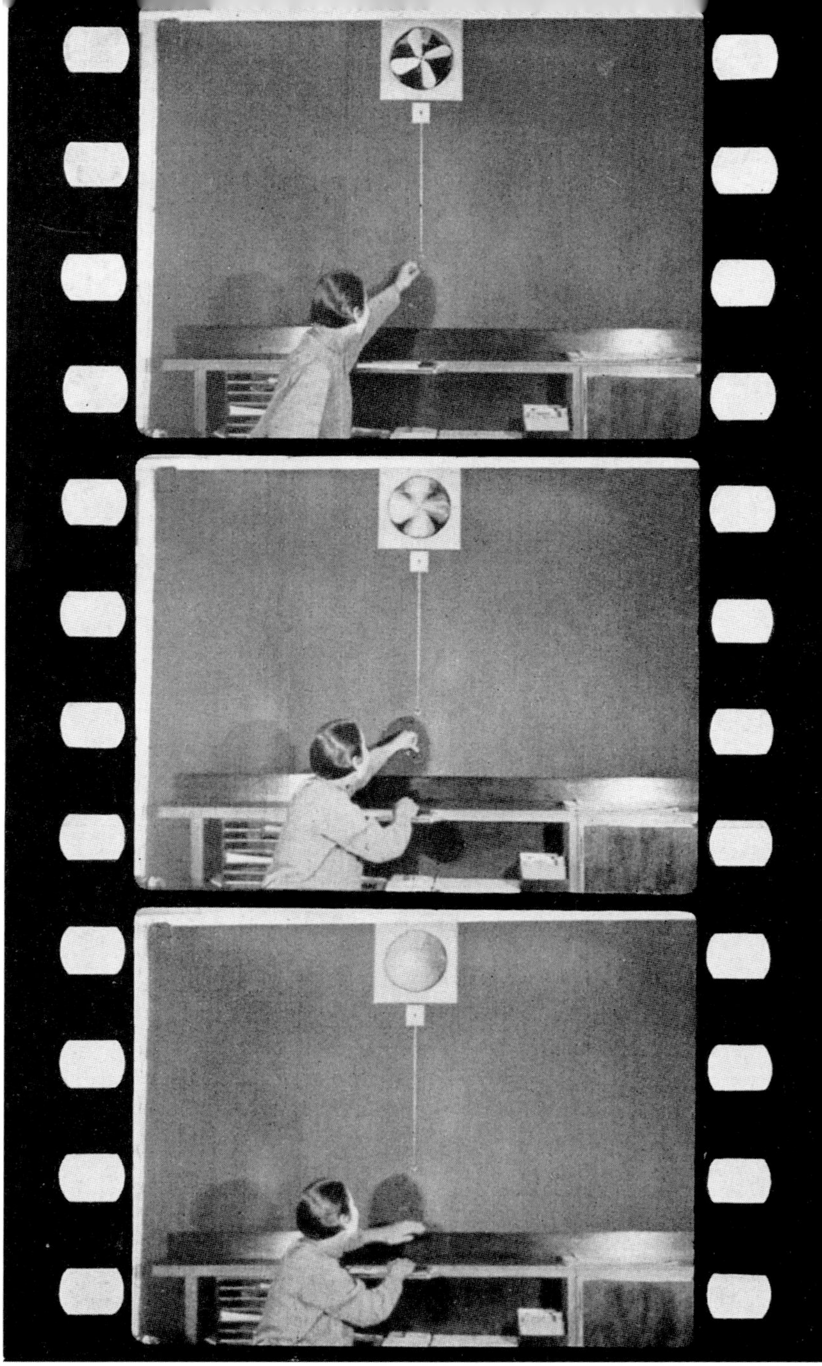

humboldt-film / berlin

**fig. 103** bauhaus masters' apartments
fan in the living room of gropius's detached house (junkers-werke)

**fig. 104** **bauhaus masters' apartments**
veranda outside the dining room of gropius's detached house
the western opening (on the right side of the picture) is protected against wind by an undivided fixed plate glass pane

photo lucia moholy / berlin

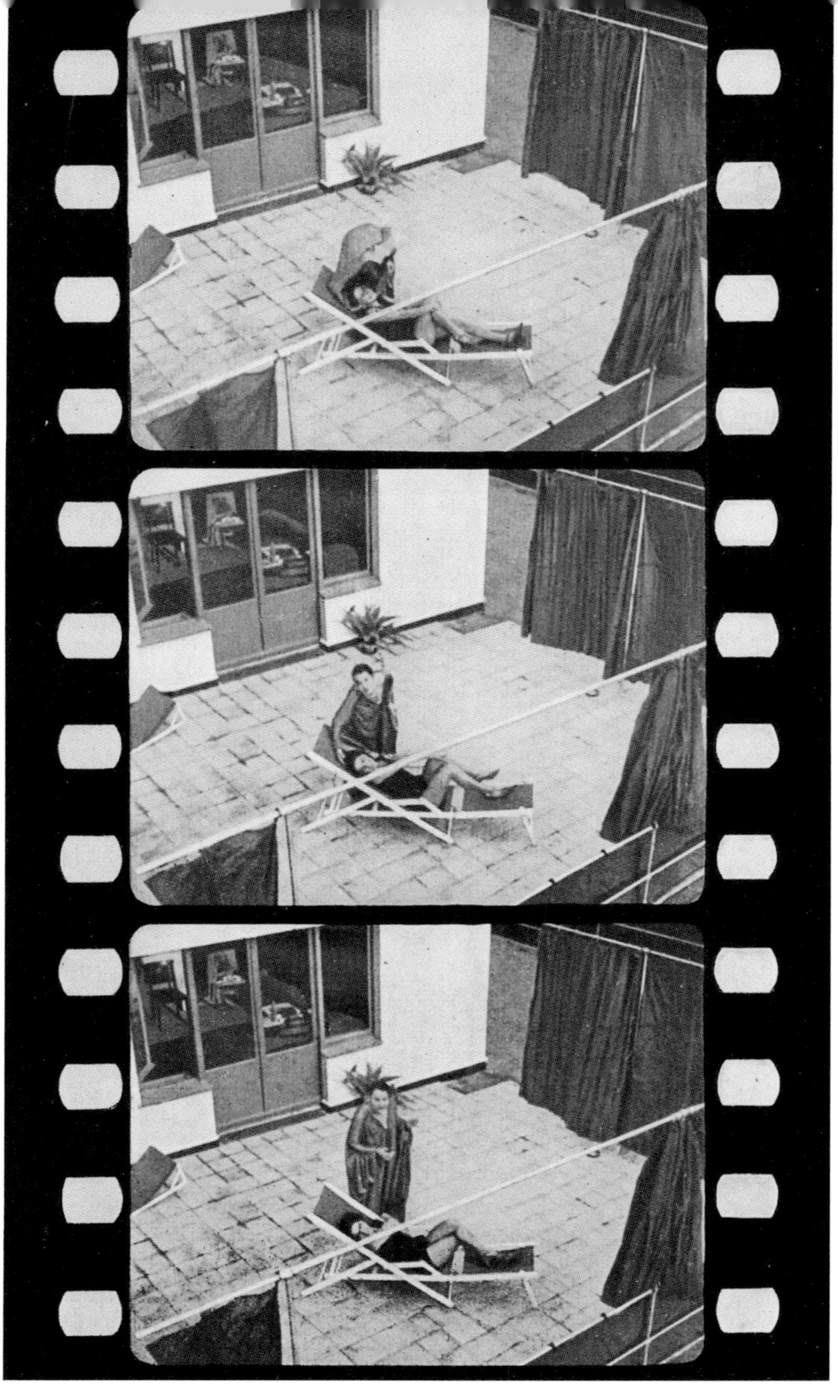

humboldt-film / berlin

**fig. 105** bauhaus masters' apartments
roof terrace on the upper floor of gropius's detached house

**fig. 106** **bauhaus masters' apartments**
bedroom in gropius's detached house
built-in cupboards: w. gropius and m. breuer
color design: m. breuer and bauhaus mural painting department
the entire wall between this and the adjoining room is composed of deep cupboards and alcoves (built-in wooden fixtures) (see floor plan, fig. 79)

photo lucia moholy / berlin

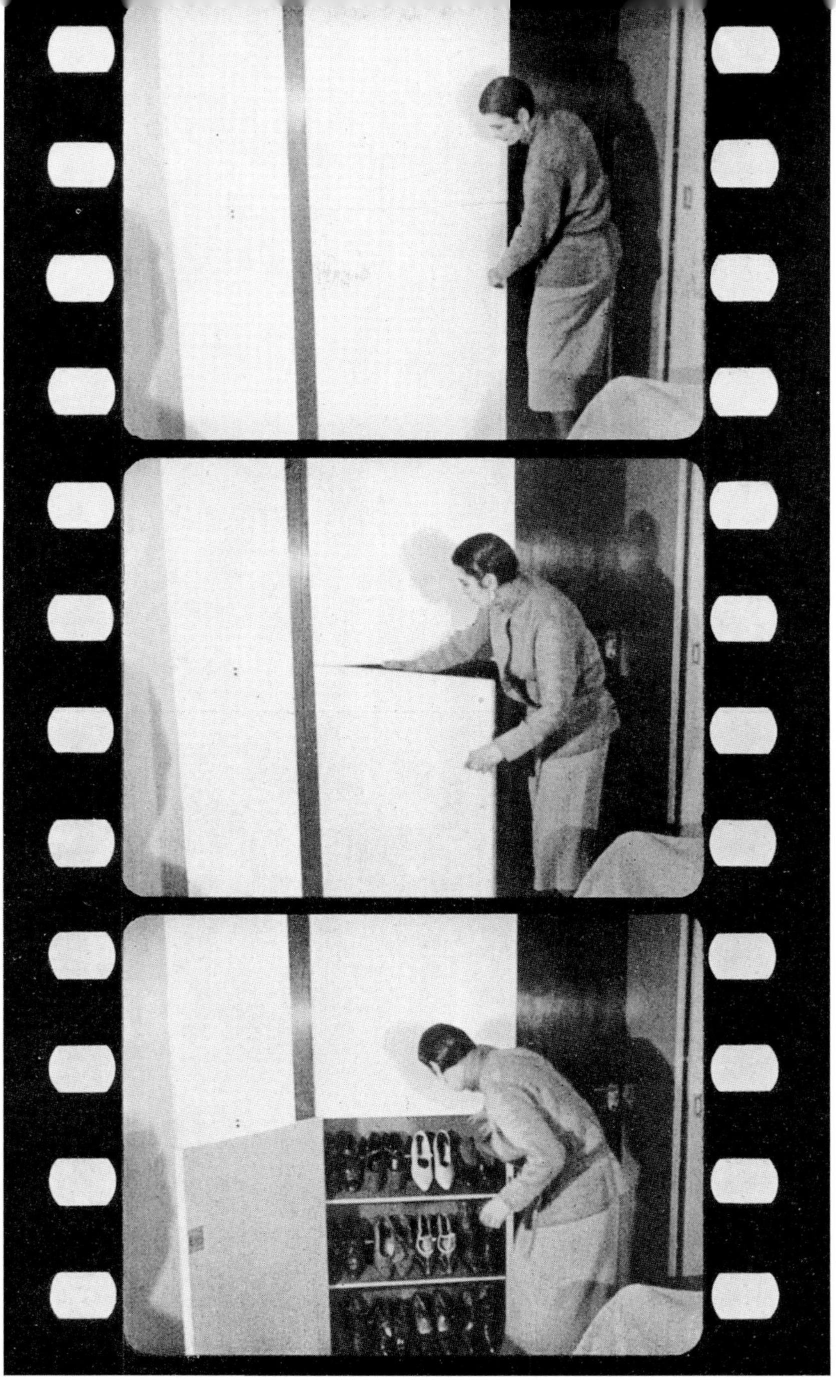

humboldt-film / berlin

**fig. 107** bauhaus masters' apartments
shoe cabinet in the bedroom of gropius's detached house

**fig. 108** **bauhaus masters' apartments**
bedside table in the bedroom of gropius's detached house

photo lucia moholy / berlin

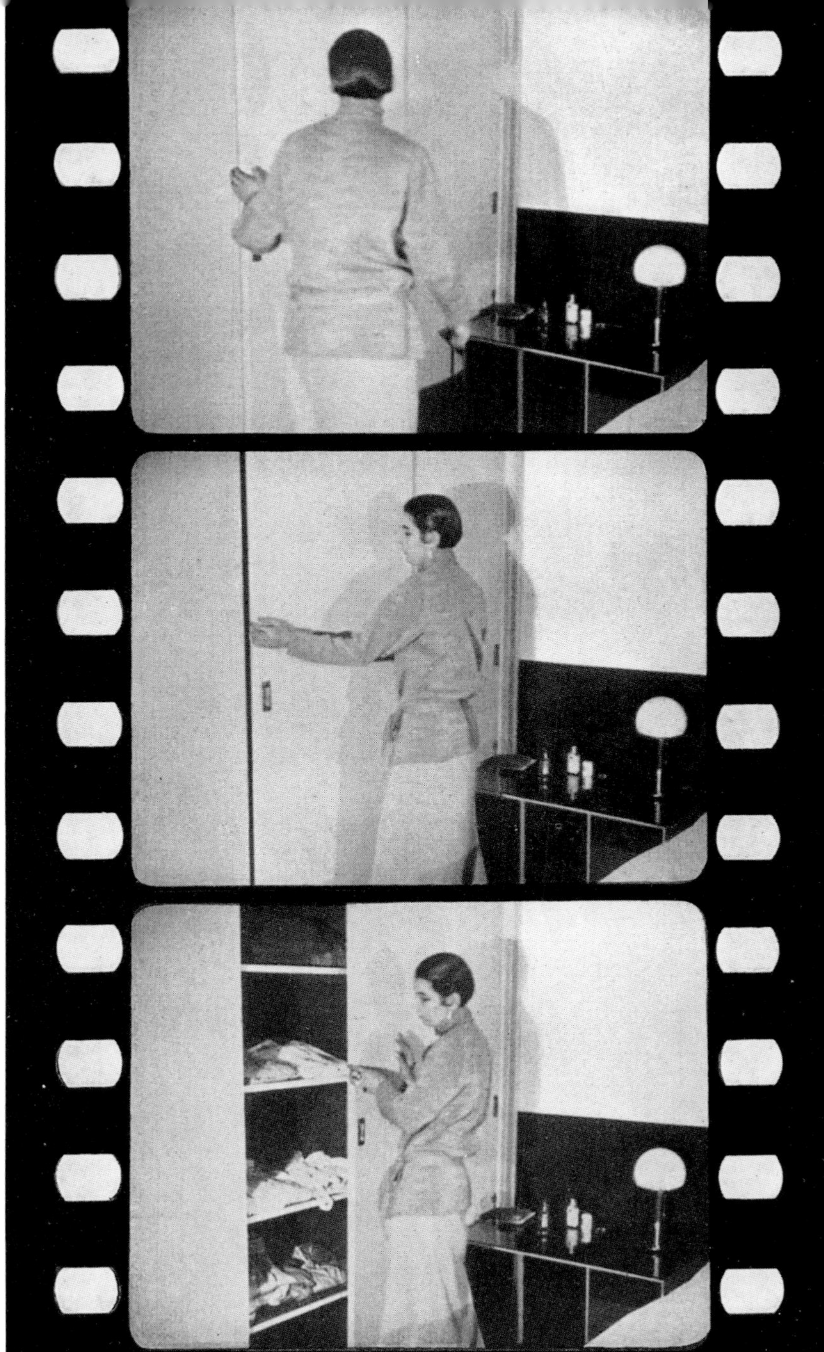

humboldt-film / berlin

**fig. 109** bauhaus masters' apartments
built-in laundry cupboard in the main bedroom of gropius's detached house

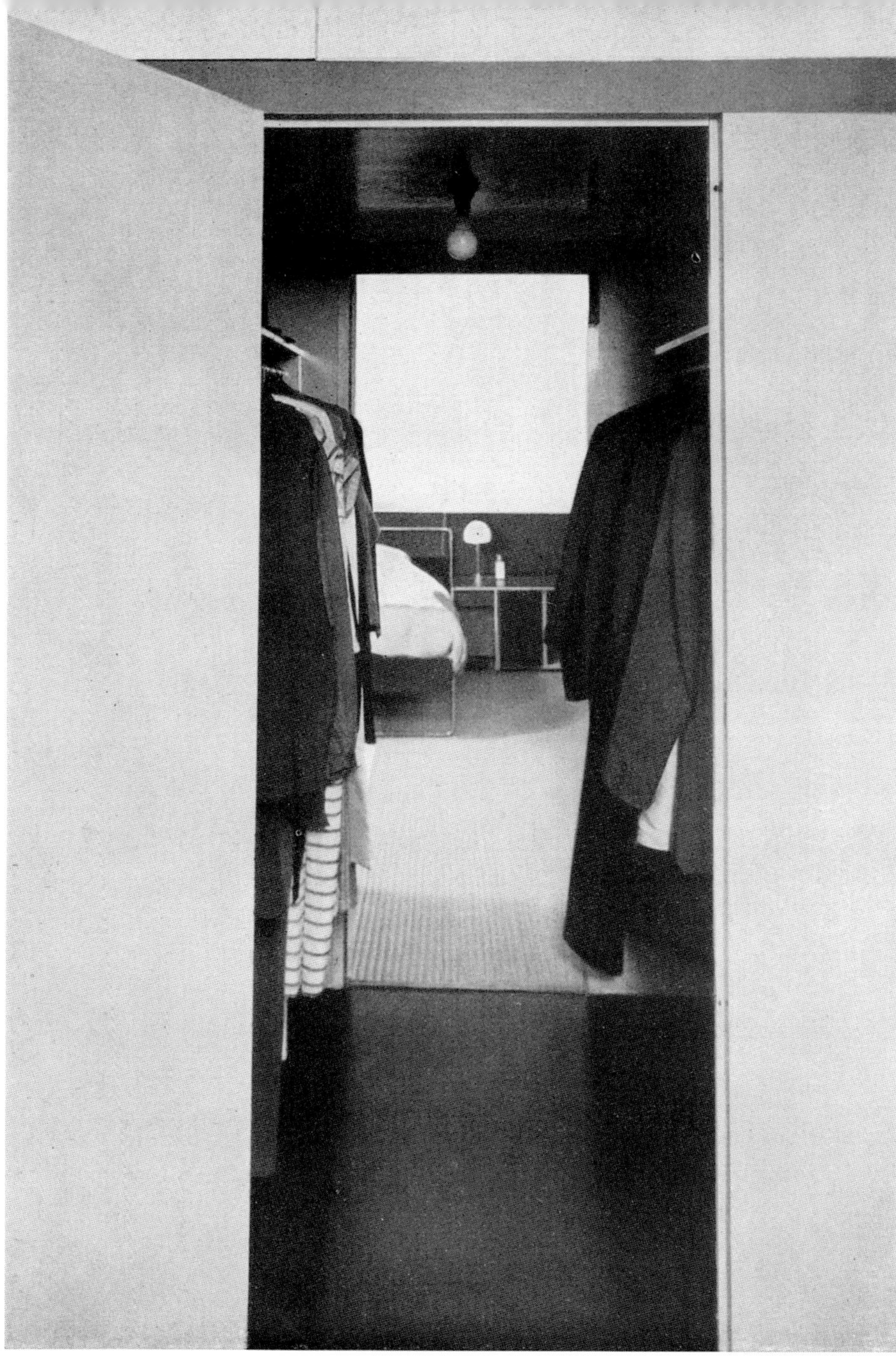

photo lucia moholy / berlin

**fig. 110** **bauhaus masters' apartments**
built-in walk-in wardrobe between two bedrooms in gropius's detached house
the light switches on and off automatically when the door is opened or closed

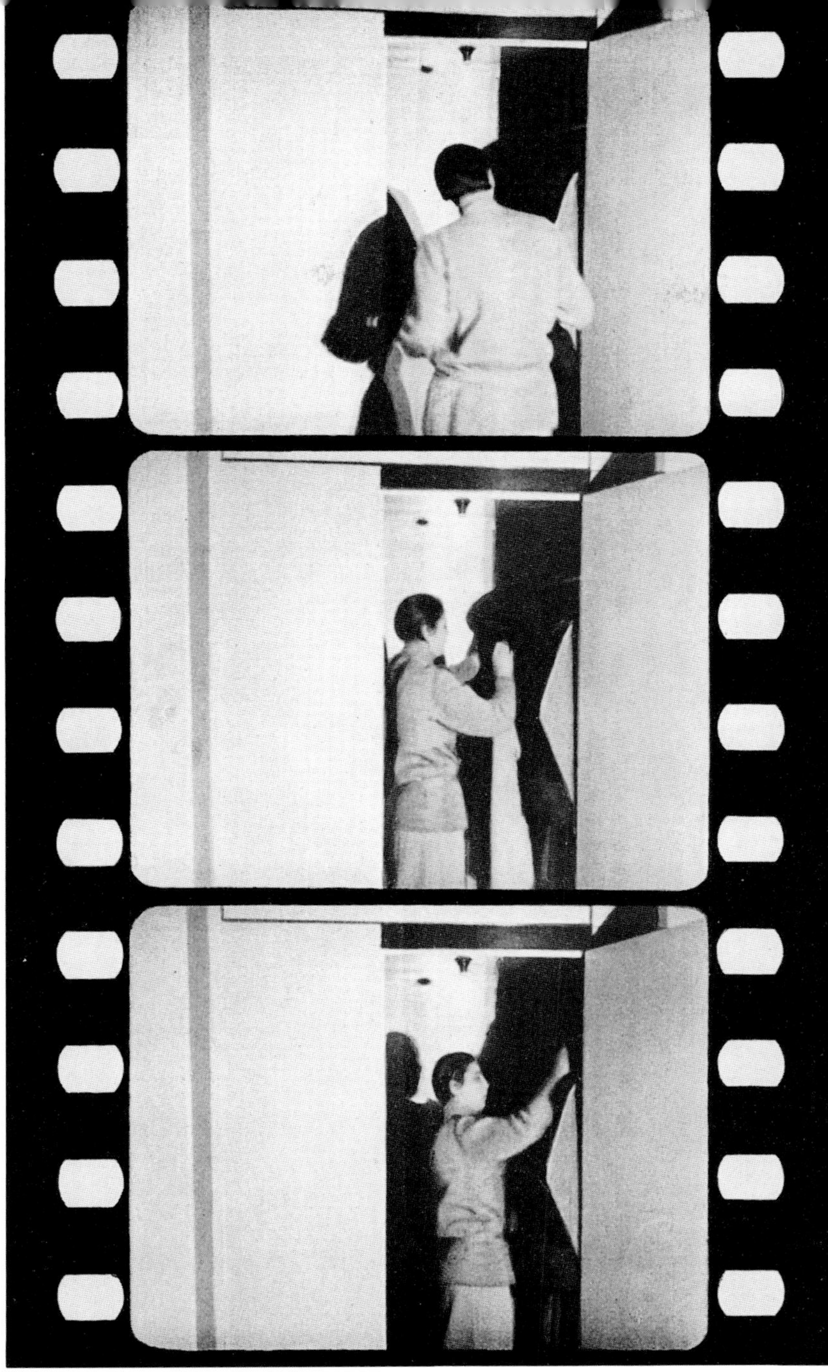

humboldt-film / berlin

**fig. 111** bauhaus masters' apartments
walk-in wardrobe in gropius's detached house (see fig. 110)

photo lucia moholy / berlin

**fig. 112** bauhaus masters' apartments
washing facilities in a bedroom in gropius's detached house

photo lucia moholy / berlin

**fig. 113** bauhaus masters' apartments
mirror-lined alcove for personal grooming in the guest room of gropius's detached house

**fig. 114** **bauhaus masters' apartments**
scullery in gropius's detached house and view into the kitchen

photo lucia moholy / berlin

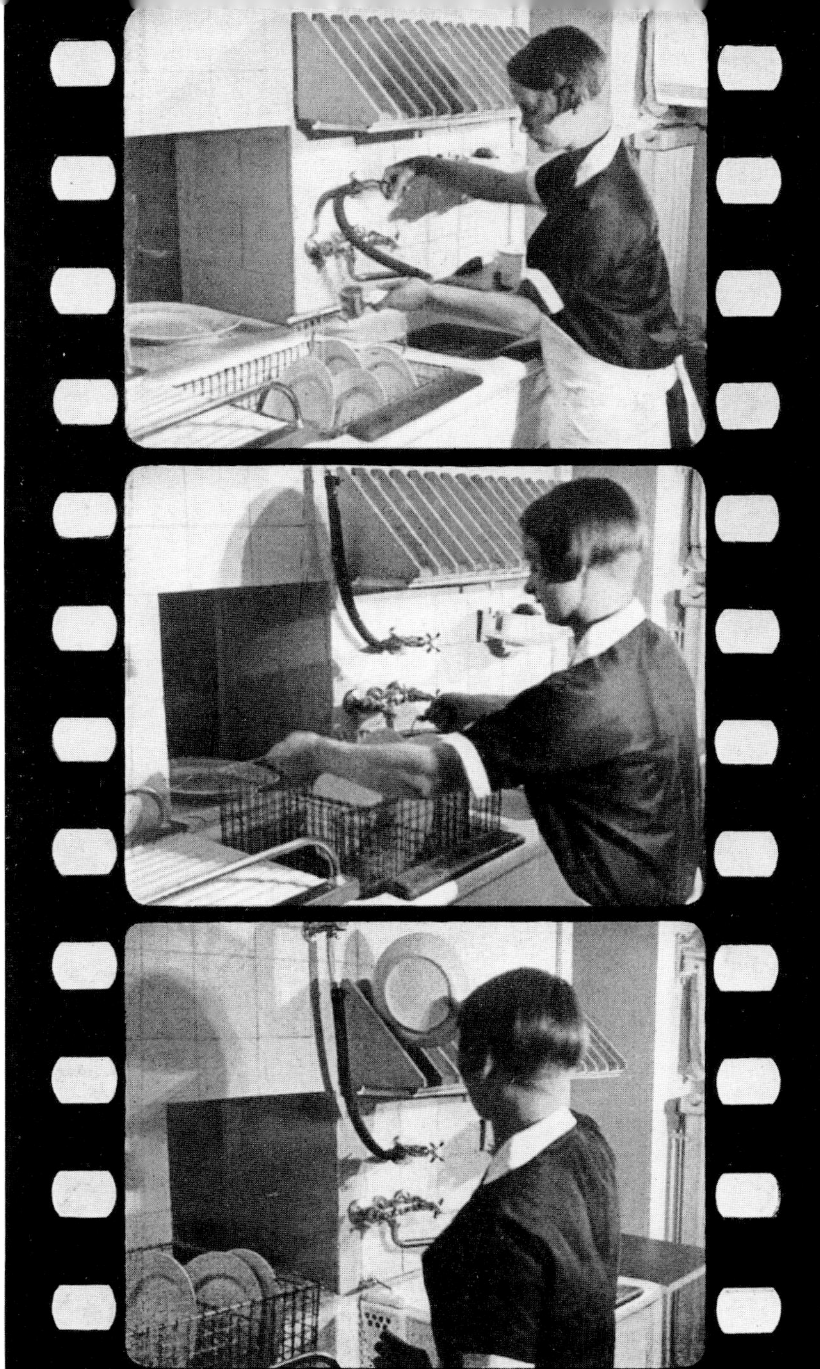

humboldt-film / berlin

**fig. 115** **bauhaus masters' apartments**
scullery in gropius's detached house
hot-water high-pressure spray; dish rack; in-cabinet plate drainer

**fig. 116 bauhaus masters' apartments**
kitchen in gropius's detached house with hatch through to the scullery
kitchen cupboard: m. breuer

photo lucia moho y / dessau

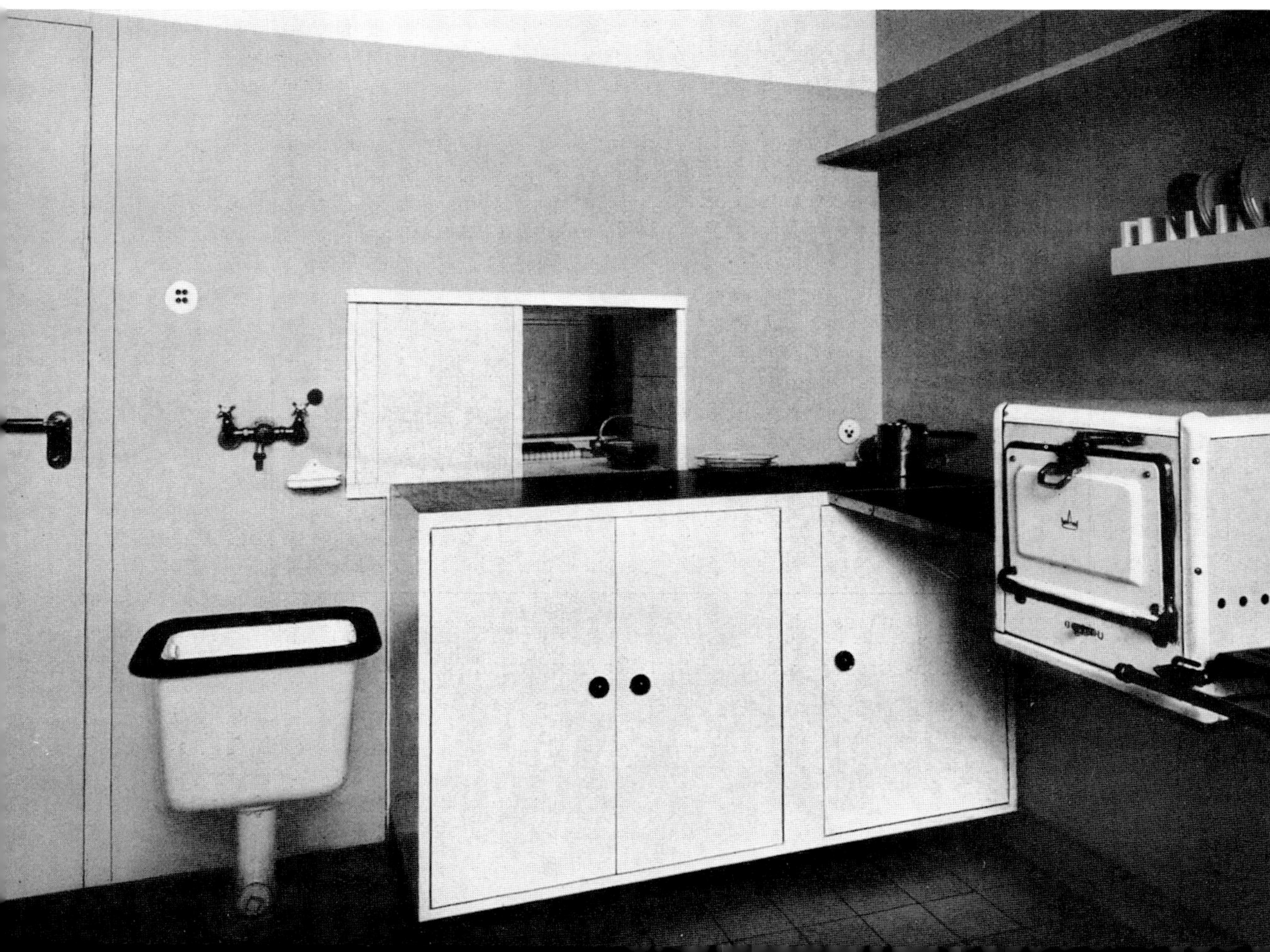

humboldt-film / berlin

**fig. 117** bauhaus masters' apartments
built-in cupboard for crockery and cutlery between dining room and scullery, can be opened from both sides (w. gropius and m. breuer)

**fig. 118 bauhaus masters' apartments**
kitchen in gropius's detached house
cupboards: m. breuer

photo lucia moholy / berlin

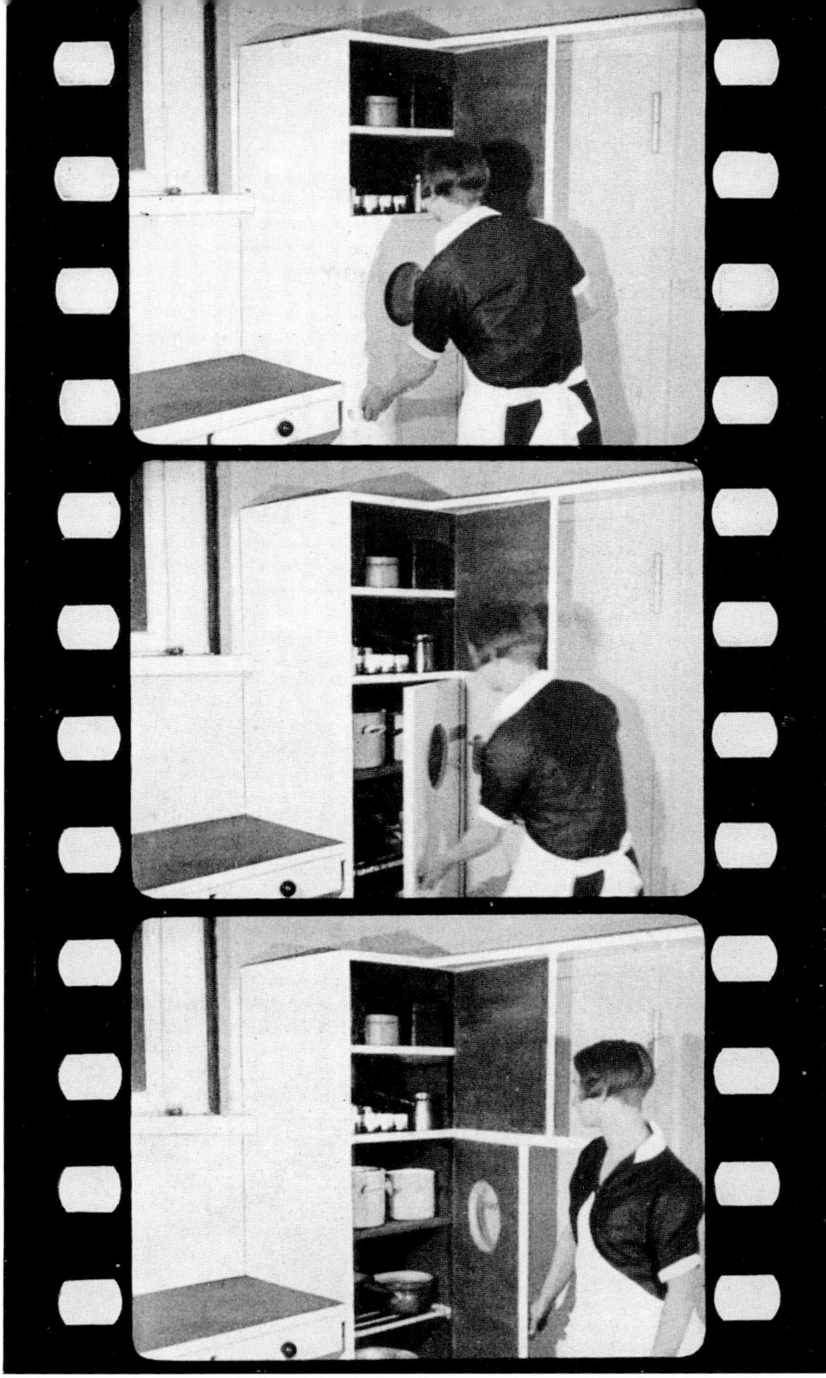

humboldt-film / berlin

**fig. 119** **bauhaus masters' apartments**
pan cupboard with galvanized grids in the kitchen of gropius's detached house (m. breuer)

**fig. 120** **bauhaus masters' apartments** photo lucia moholy / berlin
cupboard for ironing board and iron in gropius's detached house
the combined photo shows the board folded out and folded away at the same time

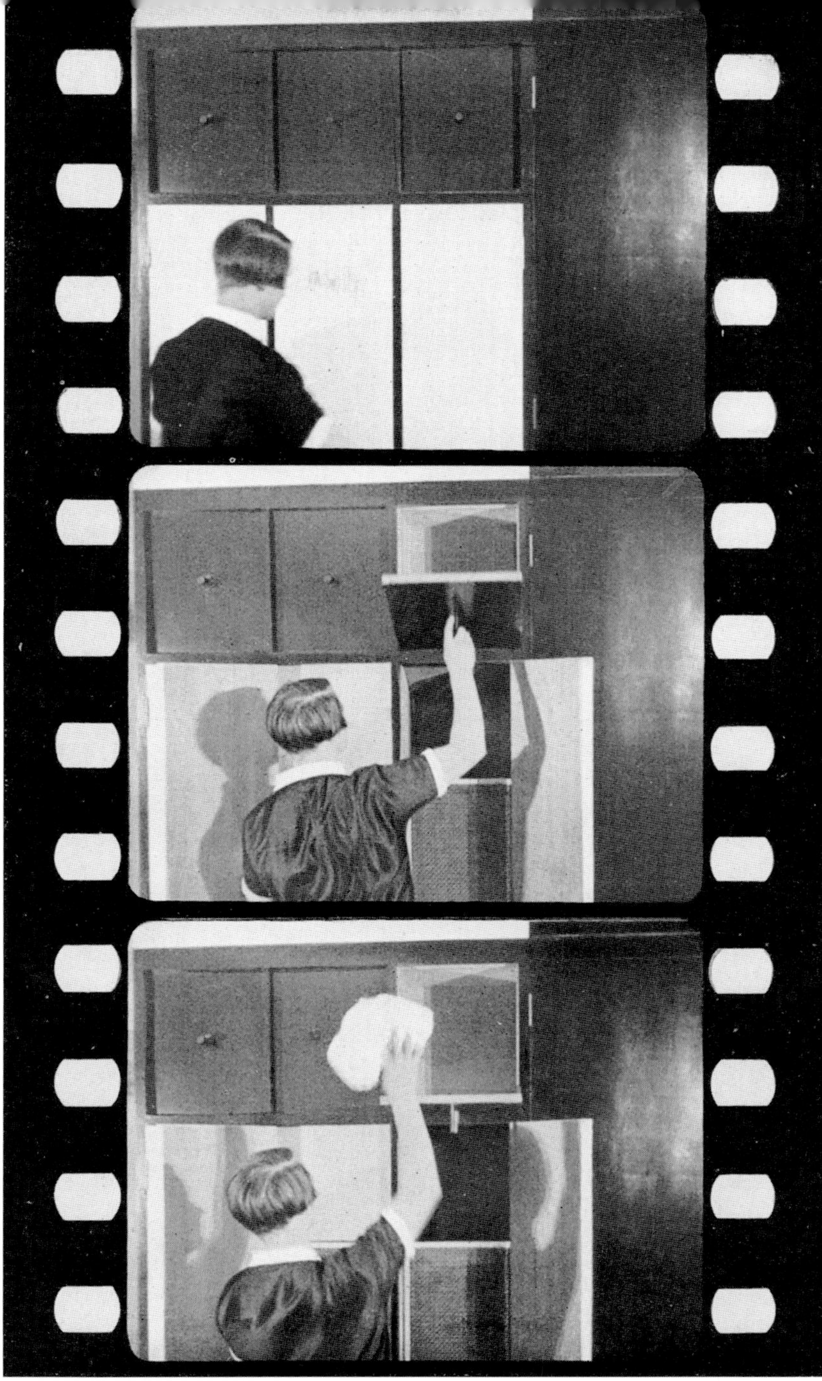

**fig. 121** bauhaus masters' apartments humboldt-film / berlin
three-part built-in cupboard for dirty laundry in the staircase of gropius's detached house
the cupboard is ventilated to the exterior through the wall, separate compartments for table linen, bed linen and underclothes

**fig. 122** **bauhaus masters' apartments**
bathroom in gropius's detached house
the walls are covered with crystal glass panels

photo lucia moholy / berlin

photo lucia moholy / berlin

**fig. 123** bauhaus masters' apartments
laundry on the 1st floor of gropius's detached house
drum washer and drying centrifuge with beltless motor drive
drum washer heated with gas

photo lucia moholy / berlin

**fig. 124** bauhaus masters' apartments
east view of a semidetached house seen from the roof of the detached house. terraces and projecting balconies on all floors, direct access to the exterior from almost all rooms
the balconies are formed by unsupported cantilevered portions of the solid ceilings

**fig. 125** **bauhaus masters' apartments**
east view of a semidetached house

the sense of space is changing; while the old era of now-concluded cultural developments embodied a heavy earthbound character in solid, monolithic-looking structures and individualized interiors, work by today's seminal architects reveals an altered sense of space, which reflects the movement, the communication of our time in more supple built structures and spaces, while seeking to maintain the connection between the interior and the surroundings that enclosing walls negate.

photo lucia moholy / berlin

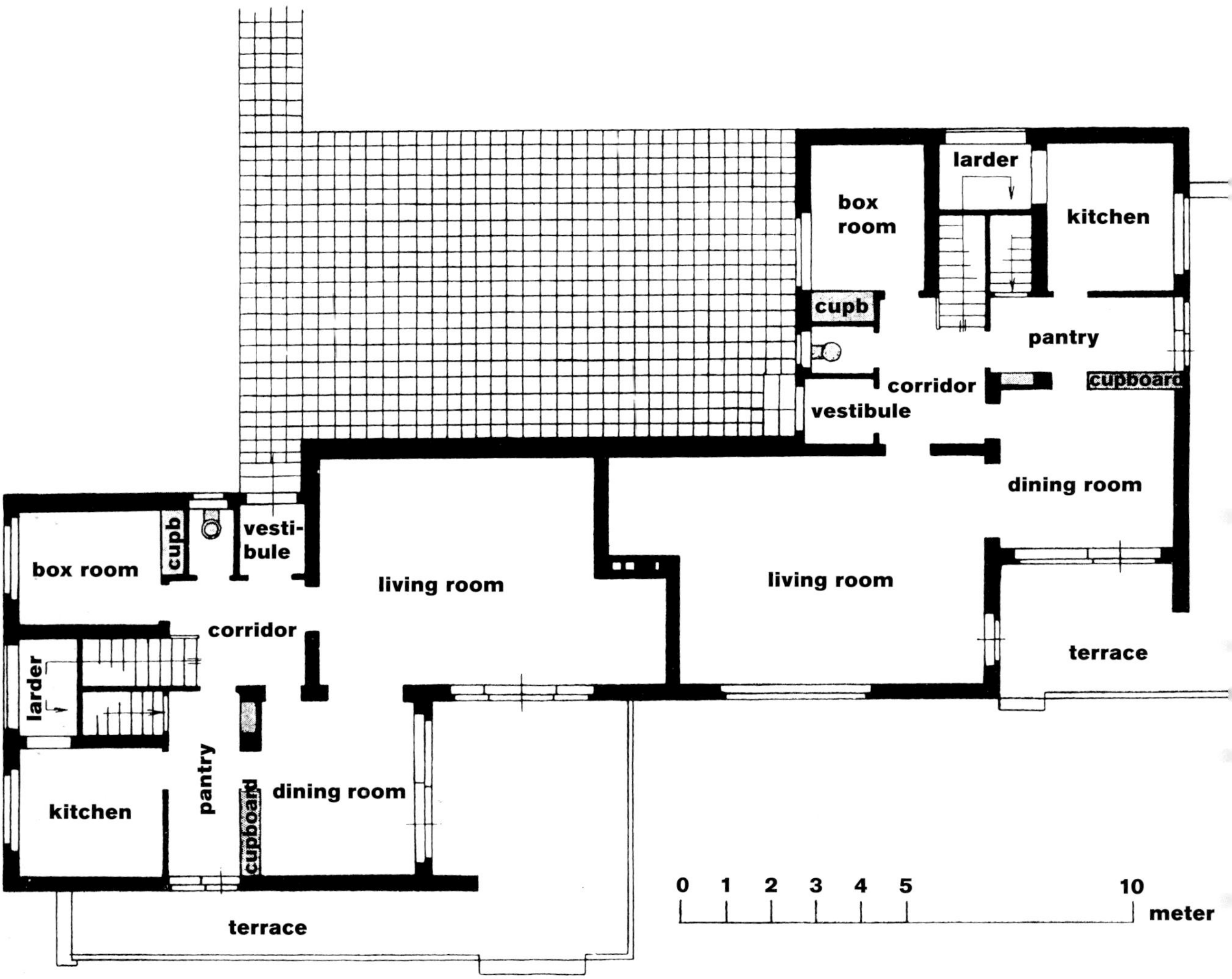


**fig. 126** bauhaus masters' apartments
ground-floor floor plan of a semidetached house
the floor plan of each of the two apartments is the mirror image of the other, rotated 90° from east to south. therefore:
use of ident cal components but different views; greater privacy

the size of the rooms can be reduced without detriment to the design in order to enhance the residents' comfort. the increasing difficulties concerning domestic staff, which e.g. in america already makes measures for an altered lifestyle essential, are a decisive factor in the configuration of the organism for living in. organization and technology must save the housewife from using all her energy solely to run the household rather than having this energy freely available for her own intellectual development and for the children's upbringing.

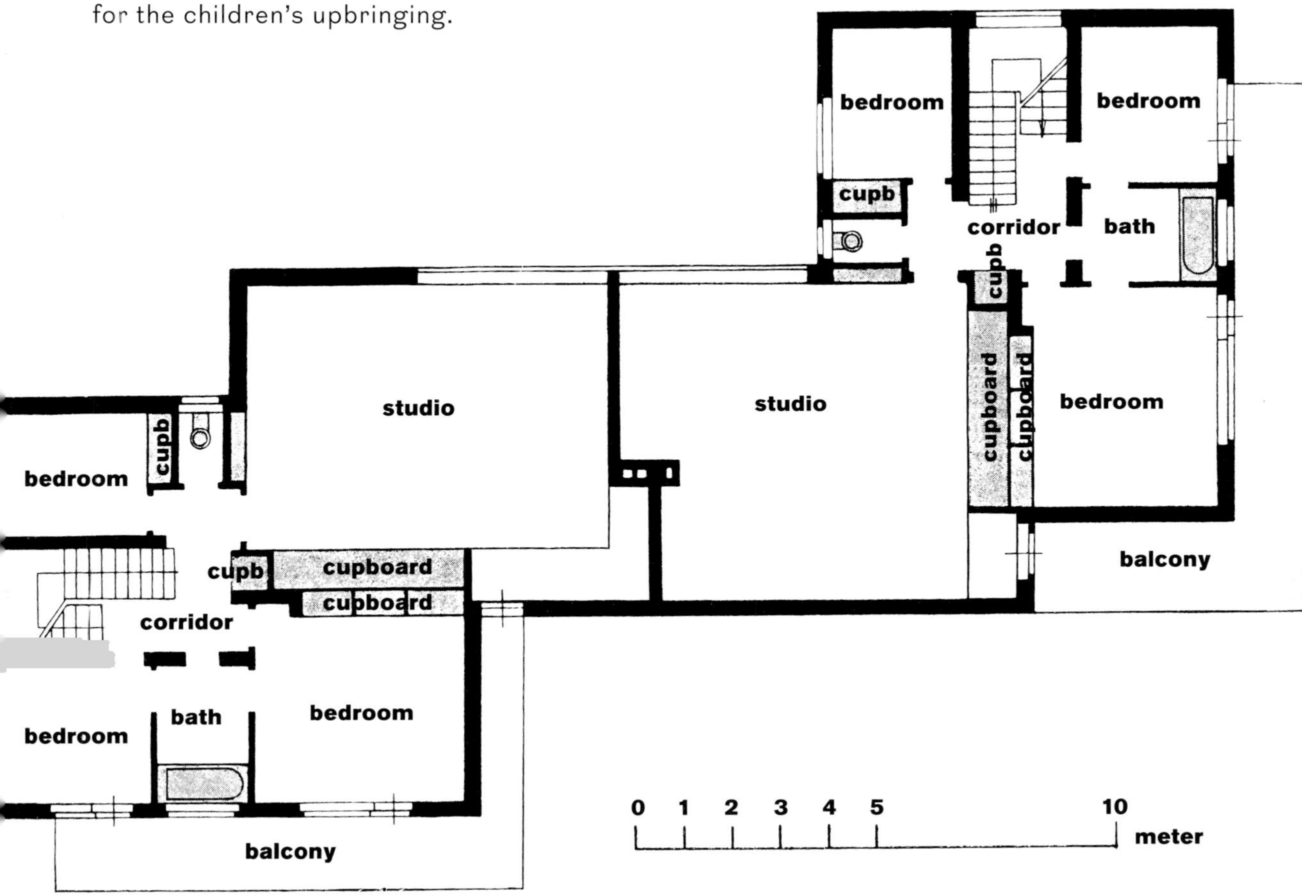


**fig. 127** bauhaus masters' apartments
upstairs floor plan of a semidetached house
the left-hand apartment also contains two bedrooms on the second floor

**fig. 128** **bauhaus masters' apartments**
seating area outside the dining rcom of the semidetached houses

photo lucia moholy / berlin

photo lucia moholy / berlin

**fig. 129** **bauhaus masters' apartments**
garden (south) view of a semidetached house

**fig. 130** **bauhaus masters' apartments**
studio in a semidetached house
(moholy-nagy's studio)

although the floor plans are identical, the variations in the color design and furnishing of the individual apartments creates such a distinctive impact that the viewer does not realize that the rooms in the various apartments are identical.

photo lucia moholy / berlin

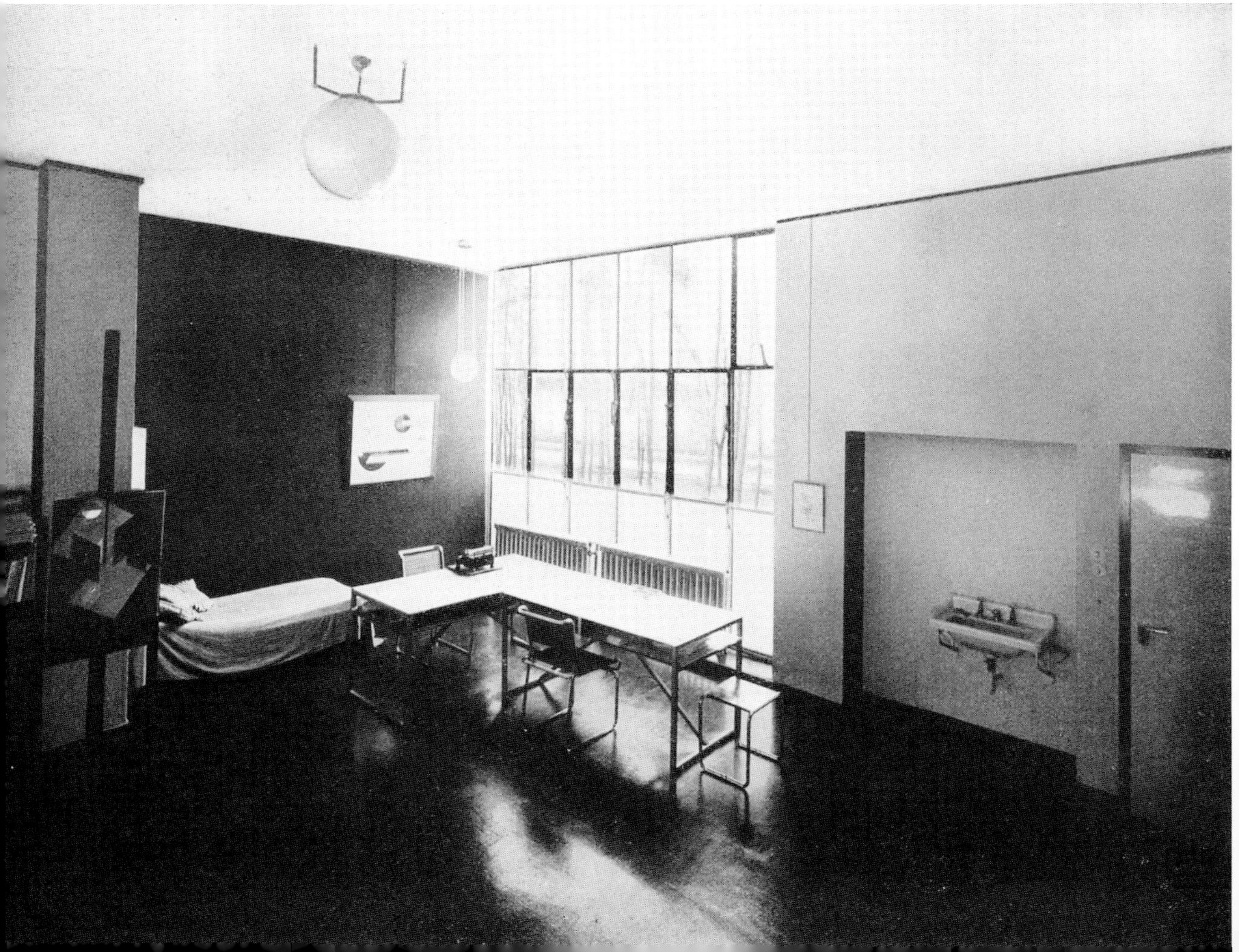

photo lucia moholy / berlin

**fig. 131** **bauhaus masters' apartments**
studio steel-framed pivot window in a semidetached house. window parapet made of eternit panels

**fig. 132** **bauhaus masters' apartments**
living room in a semidetached house
interior design: g. muche

photo consemüller / bauhaus

photo lucia moholy / berlin

**fig. 133** bauhaus masters' apartments
view from a window in a semidetached house

the housewife, who faces so many more demands in the exhausting hustle and bustle of contemporary life than in the past, and who is rarely able to obtain sufficient domestic help, will be grateful when she is no longer confronted in her home with an overwhelming abundance of useless objects and ornate furnishings, caring for which steals away her time, while they create only an old-fashioned, outdated sense of "comfort." the new apartments' advantages will be most rapidly apparent to her. just as it doesn't occur to us to cross the street in a rococo outfit instead of our modern attire, we also wish our extended apparel, the apartment, to be freed from meaningless clutter and superfluous decoration. we have grown weary of arbitrary styles, have moved from whimsy to order and are now seeking essential and meaningful expressions of our domestic surroundings in clear, concise and simple forms that correspond to the nature of our life today.

**figs. 134/135** **bauhaus masters' apartments**
living room in a semidetached house
moholy-nagy's apartment
furniture: m. breuer

photo lucia moholy / berlin

photo lucia moholy / berlin

even today we still find newly furnished apartments in rococo or renaissance style and it is almost incomprehensible that people of our current epoch allow themselves to be persuaded that this is the most desirable and "noble" framework for domestic existence. the strange gulf that this view creates in the individual between their professional need for order, practicality, speed and clarity and their emotional need for beauty and domestic coziness meant that it seemed impossible to combine the amenities of one with the comforts of the other.
architects today have broken fundamentally with this view and consider their main task to lie in meeting the needs of their own era with the means of today's technology rather than making do with feebly imitating their predecessors.

**fig. 136** bauhaus masters' apartments
dining room in a semidetached house with crockery cupboard through to scullery
color design: l. moholy-nagy and bauhaus mural painting workshop
table and seating: m. breuer
photo lucia moholy / berlin

photo lucia moholy / berlin

**fig. 137** **bauhaus masters' apartments**
open crockery cupboard between dining room and scullery in a semidetached house (see fig. 136)

**fig. 138** bauhaus masters' apartments
bedroom corner in a semidetached house (moholy-nagy)
furniture: marcel breuer

photo lucia moholy / berlin

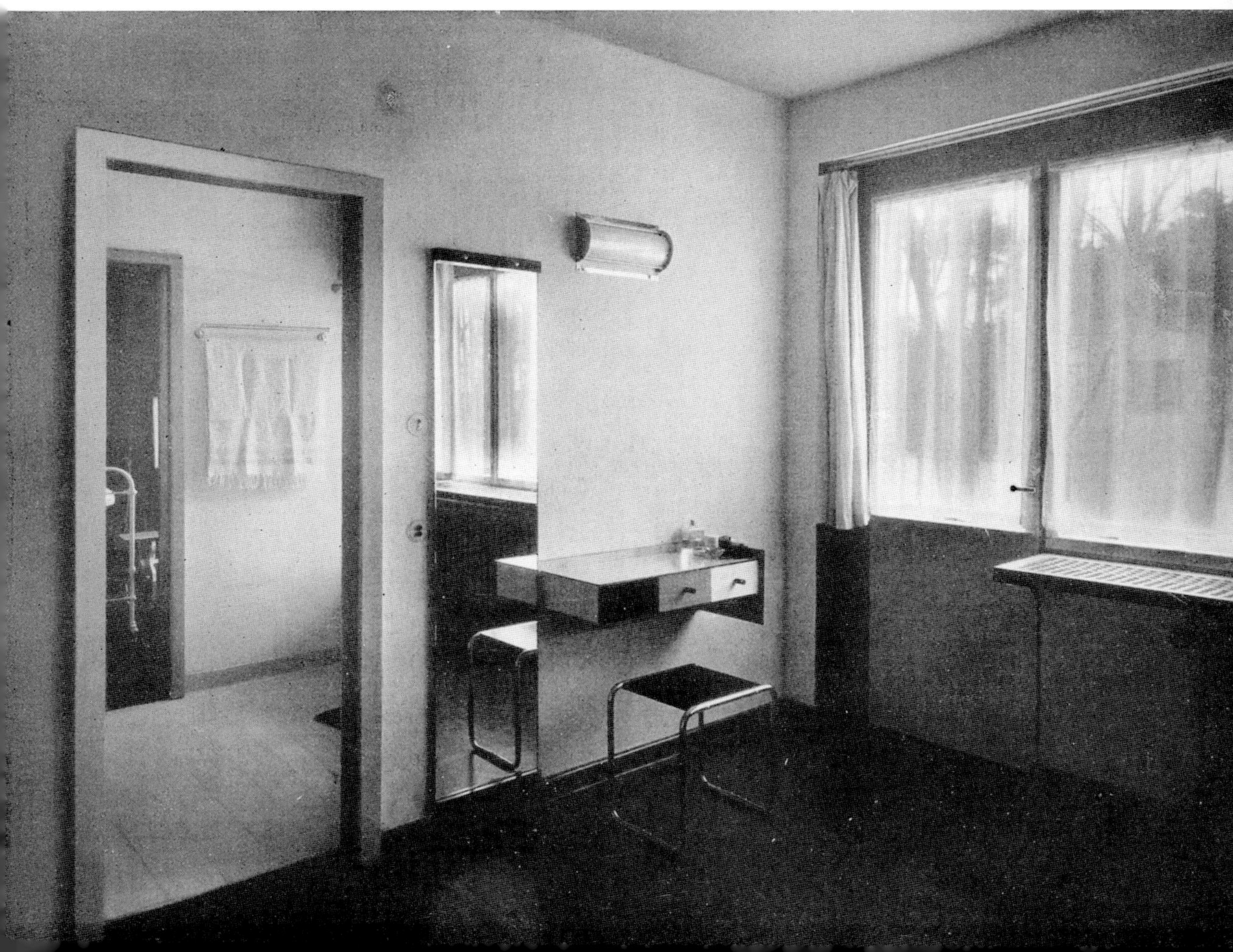

photo lucia moholy / berlin

**fig. 139** bauhaus masters' apartments
bedroom window (east) of a semidetached house

**fig. 140** **bauhaus masters' apartments**
bathroom on the 1st floor of a semidetached house

photo lucia moholy / berlin

**fig. 141** bauhaus masters' apartments photo lucia moholy / berlin
food cupboard in the kitchen, with the larder beyond, accessible from the landing on the cellar stairs

**dessau-törten estate and**
**konsumverein dessau building**
**architect: walter gropius**
**built in 1926—28**

**the city of dessau,**

on a site acquired by the state of anhalt on the main road to leipzig near the village of törten, has built

**a housing estate under the reichsheimstätte scheme**

according to my plans and under my direction for the entire project.

in 3 construction phases so far in 1926, 1927, 1928, 316 single-family terraced housing units were constructed there under the reichsheimstätte scheme, each with 5 or 4 rooms.

**this project**

aimed to reduce the rent for the houses by combining all possible rationalization options. this goal of lower rents was achieved by economic configuration of the plans, timely work preparation, careful tendering and the choice of an economical structural principle.

all the plans were drawn up on a scale of 1:20 before the tenders were awarded for the work, so that the dimensions and layout of the conduits for all the installations — gas, water, lighting, heating — were stipulated from the outset.

given the number of housing units constructed simultaneously,

1926 60 houses
1927 100 houses
1928 156 houses

the use of large-scale equipment was rational. in this case, cranes weighing approx. 1.5 t were used to move the construction units.

surveying the building site revealed the presence of plentiful good-quality construction sand and gravel. consequently, i decided to use a concrete construction method according to my own system for the buildings, in order to ensure that the volume of material to be transported to the building site remained low, because the presence of gravel and sand meant that only cement and annealed coke slag would need to be transported for production of the slag-concrete wall units.

### the construction principle of the terraced houses:

load-bearing firewalls of slag-concrete hollow blocks of 22.5/25/50 cm, that is, of a scale that allows them to be positioned by one man. ceilings freely suspended from firewall to firewall with precast concrete joists, dry-laid without intermediate filling, beam to beam. the front walls are formed by insulating, non-load-bearing panels of hollow slag-concrete blocks supported by reinforced-concrete cantilevered beams, with direct load transfer to the firewalls.

### the implementation

the structural work was carried out on the basis of a previously elaborated detailed site plan in such a way that the construction units, wall elements and concrete ceiling beams were produced on the construction site using machines as if on an assembly line, with processes planned to limit idling time and inefficiency.

behind the row of houses to be built, eight block-casting machines were used to produce the hollow-core slag blocks in a piecework system. the output of two men gradually increased to up to 250 units per day. after the material for a group of 8 houses was ready and stored in stacks, the 8 machines were moved on to the next group of houses and so on.

the precast concrete joists were produced using high-quality cement in a piecework system at one end of the construction site in machines built for this purpose, the metal reinforcing bars were prepared adjacent to them on workbenches as an extension of the production line. the unset joists exit the machine onto a drying table, at the end of which the joists that have already set are transferred by mining trolley to the crane, which moves the joists in bundles of six units.

the principle for the work on the construction site was to employ the same workman repeatedly for the same construction phase in each group of houses and thereby increase productivity. in order to ensure from the outset that the individual construction phases for the skeleton and the interior would intermesh, a precise schedule, along the lines of a railway timetable, was drawn up, initially on a theoretical basis before construction began, with additions to the finished plan during construction in keeping with on-site developments. this timetable makes it possible to attain an overview at a glance of how the various work processes intermesh and to adopt measures in a timely manner.

this working method and structural principle made it possible to achieve the following production times:

in the 1928 construction period, in 88 working days, 130 houses including production of all construction components and building blocks on the construction site as skeleton structure ready-plastered inside and outside, i.e. 0.67 days per house unit or 5 1/2 working hours per house unit.

**the layout of the individual rooms**

can be seen on the floor plan. as these are semirural housing estates with 350—400 sqm of land per house unit, only water from the kitchen and drainage water from the roof enters the wastewater system, whereas the toilet facilities were designed as peat toilets in order to reutilize toilet waste in the kitchen gardens.

the houses have central heating. in the first construction period a hot-air heating system, in the second and third construction periods hot-water central heating. coal-fired stove, adjacent to it a gas connection for gas stove. all houses are equipped with bathrooms, in the first construction period with a gas connection for junkers gas-fired water heater, in the second and third construction phases with a boiler system.

the bedrooms are large enough throughout to hold 2 standard beds.

all doors are smooth plywood doors in drawn iron mannstaedt frames. the windows are double rabbeted, partly galvanized iron-framed windows with integrated ventilation flaps in the kitchens and bedrooms.

the flat roofs are protected against heat loss by a layer of cork screed or dry-laid cellular concrete panels.

**due to new experiences**

during the first phase of construction, the reichsforschungsgesellschaft für wirtschaftlichkeit im bau-und wohnungswesen granted a sum of 350 800.— for testing purposes, namely for 256 housing units per rm 1 000.— as a loan with 2% interest. in addition, it provided rm 44 800.— for construction tests and rm 50 000.— as a loan for the purchase of new machinery and equipment to improve the construction system. the client in return committed to appraising the technical and organizational results of the last two construction phases in keeping with the requirements of the reichsforschungsgesellschaft. the first part of this evaluation has now been published.●)

thanks to the funding provided by the reichsforschungsgesellschaft für wirtschaftlichkeit im bau- und wohnungswesen, it was possible to systematically test both the structural system and new material combinations with lightweight concrete types to assess their practical viability. further official evaluation results are to be published imminently by the reichsforschungsgesellschaft.

as a result of the general embrace of the implacable processes of industrialization and rationalization processes in the construction industry, the törten estate was fiercely opposed as an exponent of this movement. nevertheless, the fundamental ideas that were put into practice here have meanwhile found broad acceptance,

●) reichsforschungsgesellschaft: "bericht über die versuchssiedlung in dessau" special issue 7 / beuth verlag g. m. b. h. berlin 1929

| type | floor area sqm | enclosed volume cbm | pure construction costs including overhead costs rm | cost of roads, utilities connections and land rm |
|---|---|---|---|---|
| 1926 | 74.23 (5 rooms) | 337.62 | 8 734.90 | 1 342.10 |
| 1927 | 70.56 (5 rooms) | 315.34 | 9 043.30 | 1 456.70 |
| 1928 | 54.05 (4 rooms) | 286.13 | 8 043.30 | 1 456.70 |

as they are in keeping with the times. the numerical results from the estate are compiled in the tables below.

located in the center of the törten estate, the four-story

**cooperative building**

was built according to my plans by the konsumverein für dessau und umgegend in 1928. it has a volume of 4480 cbm and cost rm 111676.— or rm 24.9 per cbm including all ancillary costs. as well as shops on the ground floor, it contains three 3-room apartments, each with a kitchen.

| total cost or selling price rm | cost of 1 sqm floor area rm | costs for 1 cbm (only construction costs) rm | on 1 sqm floor area cbm | monthly expenditure on interest and loan repayment rm |
|---|---|---|---|---|
| 10100.— | 136.10 | 25.87 | 4.53 | 27.13 |
| 10500.— | 148.80 | 28.68 | 4.47 | 37.42 |
| 9500.— | 166.52 | 28.11 | 5.00 | 32.91 |

the building trade, which previously had an artisanal character, is gradually moving toward the industrial realm. more and more work at the mobile workshop on the building site is being replaced by the permanent industrial workshop — the factory. the once seasonal nature of construction, with all its disadvantages for employers and employees as well as for the entire national economy, is gradually giving way to permanent operation.
the fact that newer construction methods with new materials, new structural methods and new operating methods are only slowly beginning to assert themselves economically against the old artisanal masonry-construction method does not belie this development. due to the enormous scope of the areas encompassing within construction, the first step is to laboriously pave the way for rational production on the new basis.
the process of slowly replacing many artisanal methods of production of everyday items by industrial methods is only gradually spreading to the complex key trade of the construction industry; for this adaptation is of such drastic significance for the whole of economic life that the pace must be selected carefully to avoid jeopardizing existing economic groups, especially trades and crafts, by overhasty action.

junkers-luftbild dessau

**fig. 142** dessau-törten estate
first construction phase 1926 from a bird's-eye view

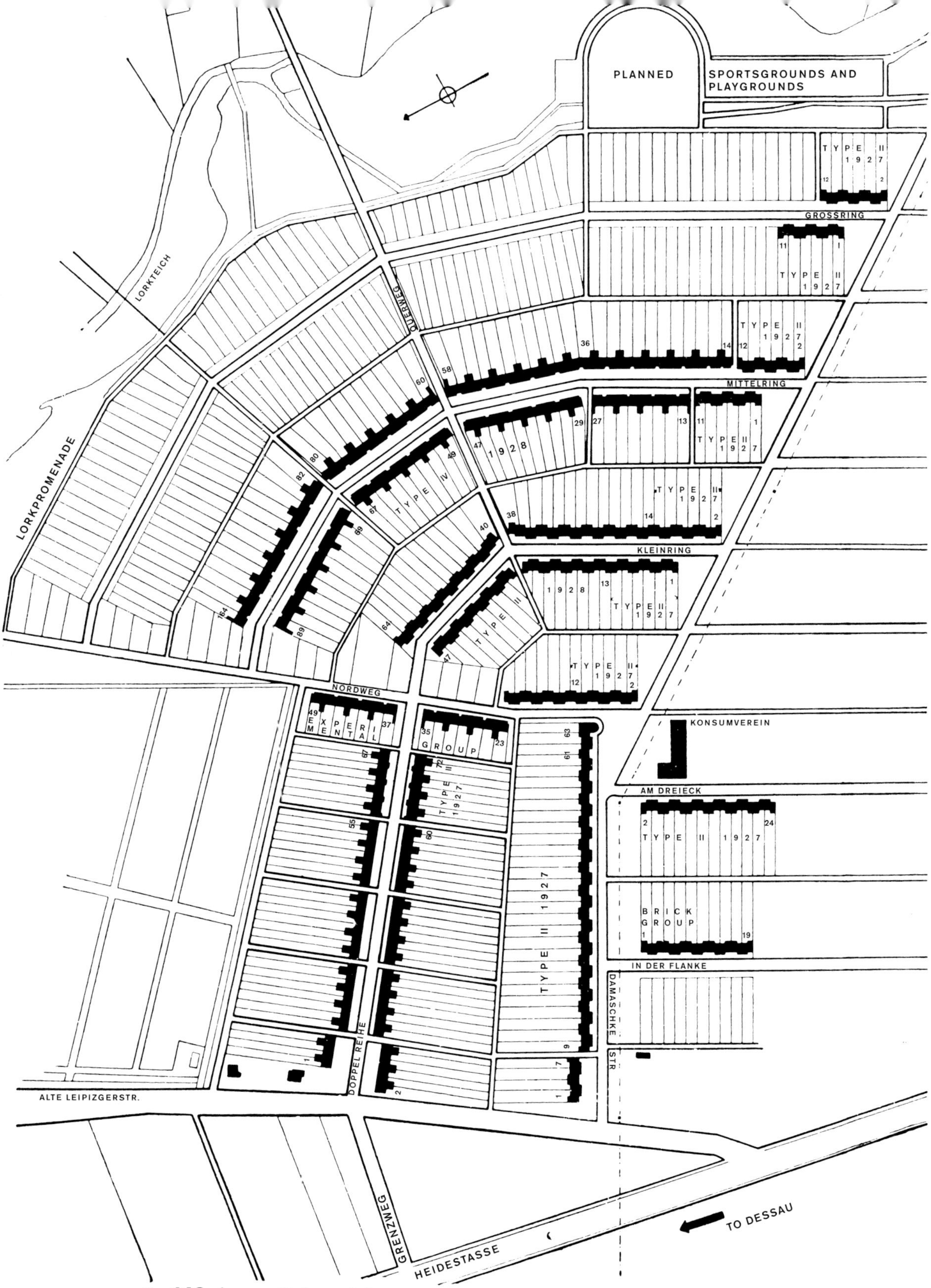


**fig. 143** dessau-törten estate
general site plan for the construction phases 1926 (60 units), 1927 (100 units), 1928 (156 units)

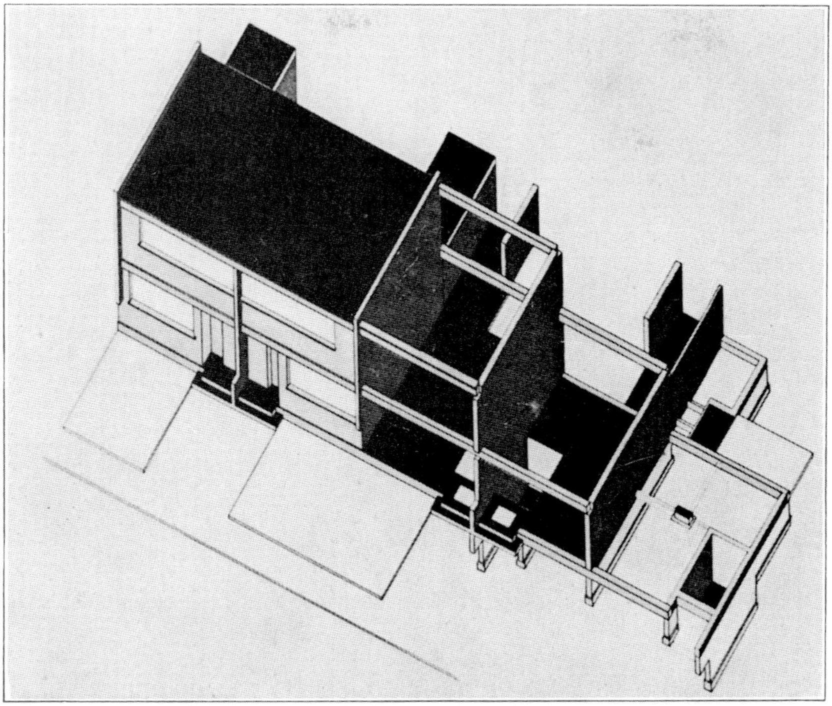

**fig. 144** **dessau-törten estate** printing block bauhaus
construction scheme, 1926 construction phase

load-bearing firewalls made of slag-concrete hollow-core bodies. ceilings, freely suspended from gable end to gable end, made of precast concrete joists, which are dry-laid beam to beam. the front walls are formed by insulating, non-load-bearing panel walls made of slag-concrete hollow-core blocks, which are supported by cantilevered reinforced-concrete beams with direct load transfer to the gable ends.

**fig. 145** **dessau-törten estate**
view of the estate from the roof of the konsumverein building to the east

the question of minimum requirements for housing is the question of the elementary minimum of space, air, light, warmth that humans need in order not to experience any constraints due to housing in fully developing their vital functions, that is, a "minimum vivendi" instead of a modus "non moriendi."●) the minimum itself changes according to the local conditions of city and country, landscape and climate; the same volume of space in a dwelling means something different in a narrow street in a big city than in a sparsely populated suburban district. von drigalski, paul vogler and other hygiene experts have found that, provided that the best possible ventilation and sunlight is available, humans need only a small amount of living space from a biological point of view, especially if the space is properly organized in terms of building technology. the comparison drawn by a well-known architect between a cleverly divided suitcase and a crate provides a vivid image of the superiority of a well-organized small modern apartment over an outdated dwelling.
however while the supply of light, sun, air and warmth is culturally more important and, with normal land prices, more economical than increasing the amount of space, the commandment must be: make windows larger, reduce the size of rooms, save on food rather than on heating. just as the value of calories in food was once overestimated to the detriment of vitamins, many people today mistakenly see the salvation of housing in larger rooms and apartments.
in accordance with more pronounced differentiation within society of each individual life in the coming era and individuals' justified aspirations to be temporarily separated from their surroundings, the ideal basic requirement will also have to be established: every adult human being will have their own room, even if it is small! the minimal apartment size resulting from these basic requirements would represent the objective minimum justified by purpose: t h e  s t a n d a r d  a p a r t m e n t.
the standardized type is not an obstacle to cultural development, but rather one of its prerequisites. it contains a selection of the best within it and separates the elementary, supraindividual from the subjective. the fairy tale of the assault of the individual through the introduction of standardized types and standardization fades away when we look back at history. the standardized type has always been a marker of a civilized social order. the recurrence of identical parts has an ordering and calming effect.
it would not occur to anyone who buys a car today to imagine having one "made to measure." here it is striking that only mass production, in other words, implementation of the standardized type on the basis of numerous standard parts, has made

●) dr. paul vogler, berlin

photo binnemann / dessau

it possible to create a relatively perfect instrument. it is impossible to comprehend why our houses should not be built according to the same rational principles, especially since proof of the reduction of costs and improvement thanks to this approach has already been provided for many other areas! the residential dwelling is a typical group structure, an element of the larger unit of the street, the city.
although the uniformity of this cell within the overall urban structure must be expressed externally, differences in size afford a much-needed variation. the best cityscapes of the past in our country or abroad provide concise proof that the beauty and clarity of a cityscape increases with implementation of the standardized type, with the repetition of typical house structures. standardization is always a final, most mature result of the consonance of objective solutions devised by various individuals. it is the common denominator of an entire era. the natural competition between different standardized types alongside each other allows the character of the individual and the nation to take effect. making building elements uniform will have the salutary consequence that our new houses and cities will again have a common character.
the standardized type is not just an invention of the present day, it has always been a sign of cultural well-being. by judiciously limiting the number of types of buildings and objects required to meet our daily needs to a mere handful, t h e i r q u a l i t y i n c r e a s e s a n d t h e i r p r i c e d e c r e a s e s, which of necessity elevates society as a whole to a higher level.

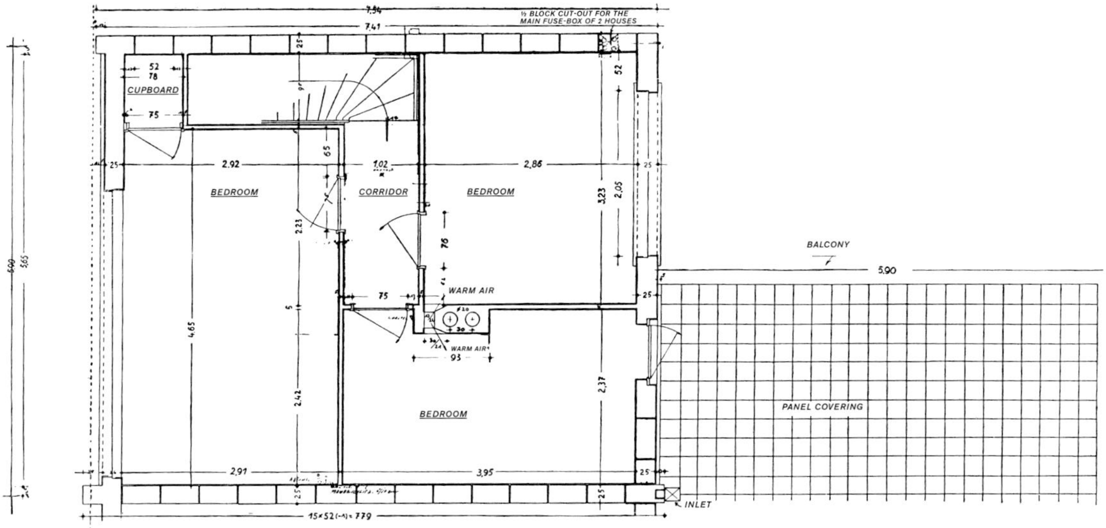


**fig. 146** dessau-törten estate
floor plan of the upper floor of the 1926 construction-phase type

printing block bauhaus

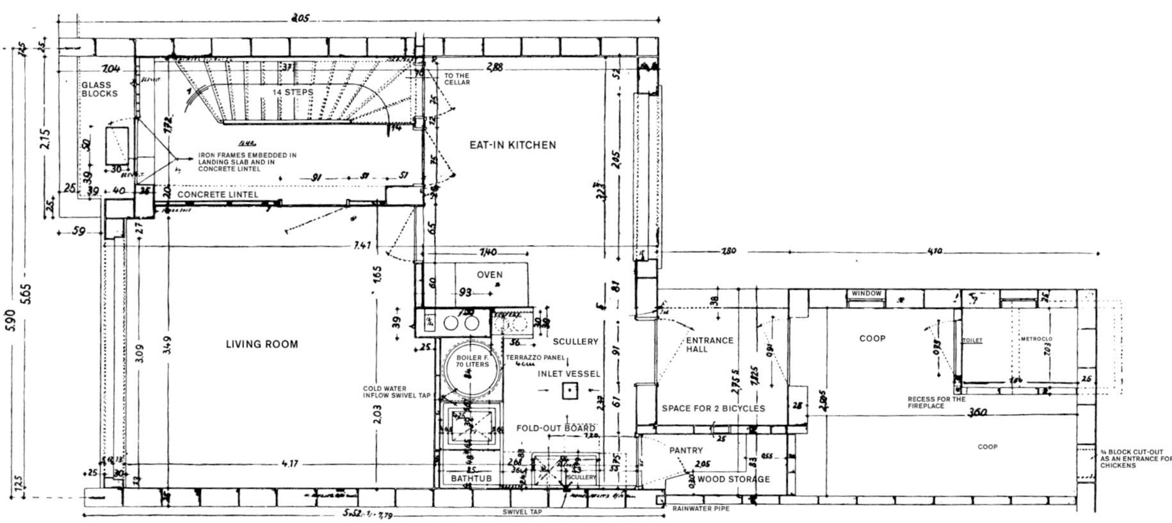


printing block bauhaus

**fig. 147** dessau-törten estate
floor plan of the ground floor of the 1926 construction-phase type

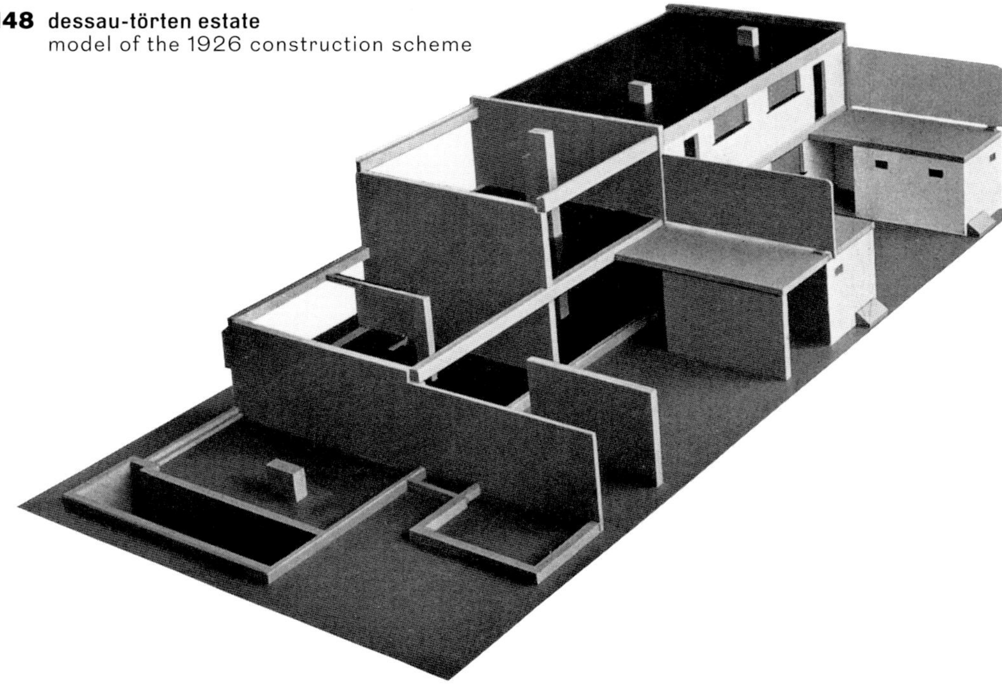

**fig. 148** dessau-törten estate
model of the 1926 construction scheme

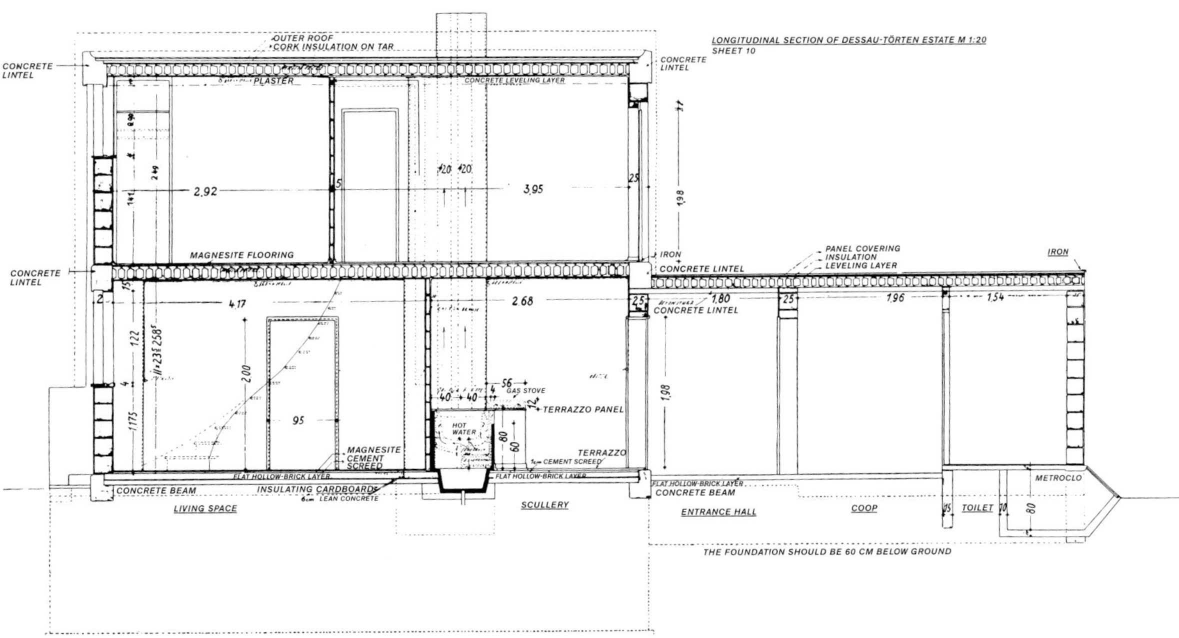


**fig. 149** dessau-törten estate
section of the 1926 type
the precast concrete ceiling joists are indicated

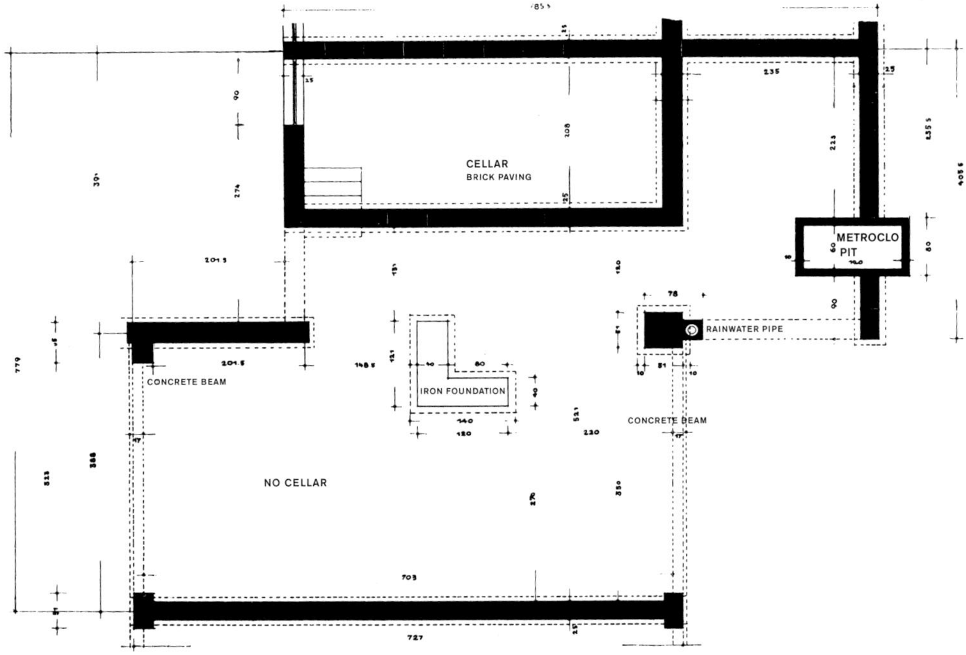


**fig. 150** dessau-törten estate
1927-type cellar and foundation floor plan

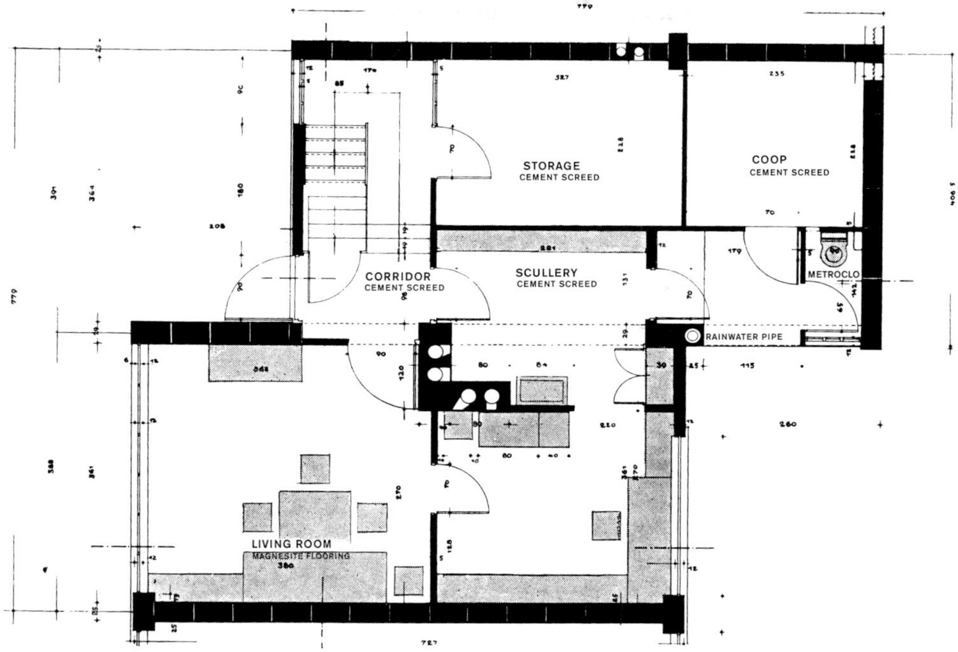


**fig. 151** dessau-törten estate
1927-type ground-floor floor plan

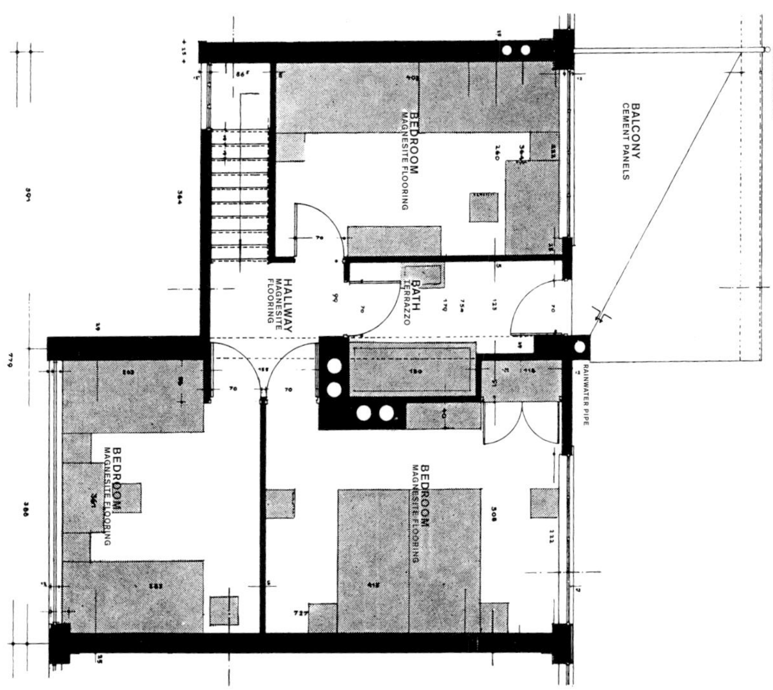


**fig. 152** dessau-törten estate
1927-type upstairs floor plan

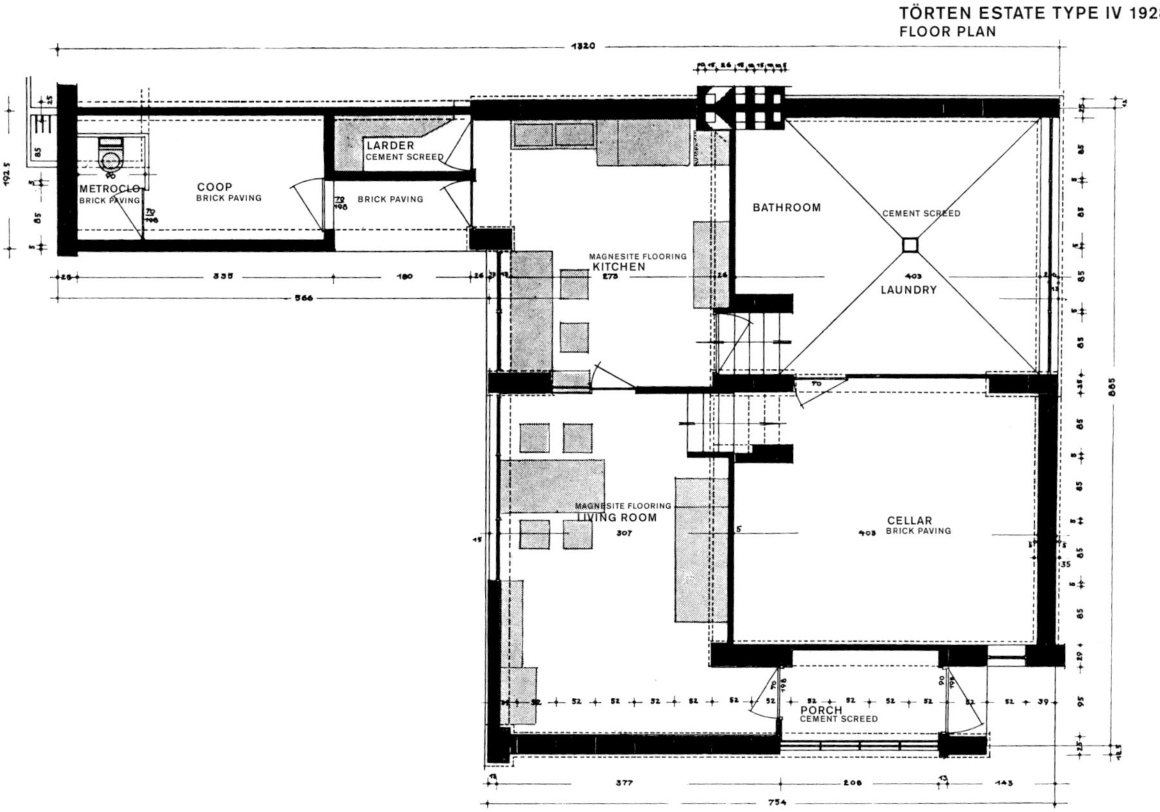


there is no doubt that a smaller, well-designed floor plan ensures greater comfort for residents than a larger, inefficient old-style floor plan.

**fig. 153** dessau-törten estate
1928-type basement and ground-floor floor plan

TÖRTEN ESTATE TYPE IV 1928
FLOOR PLAN

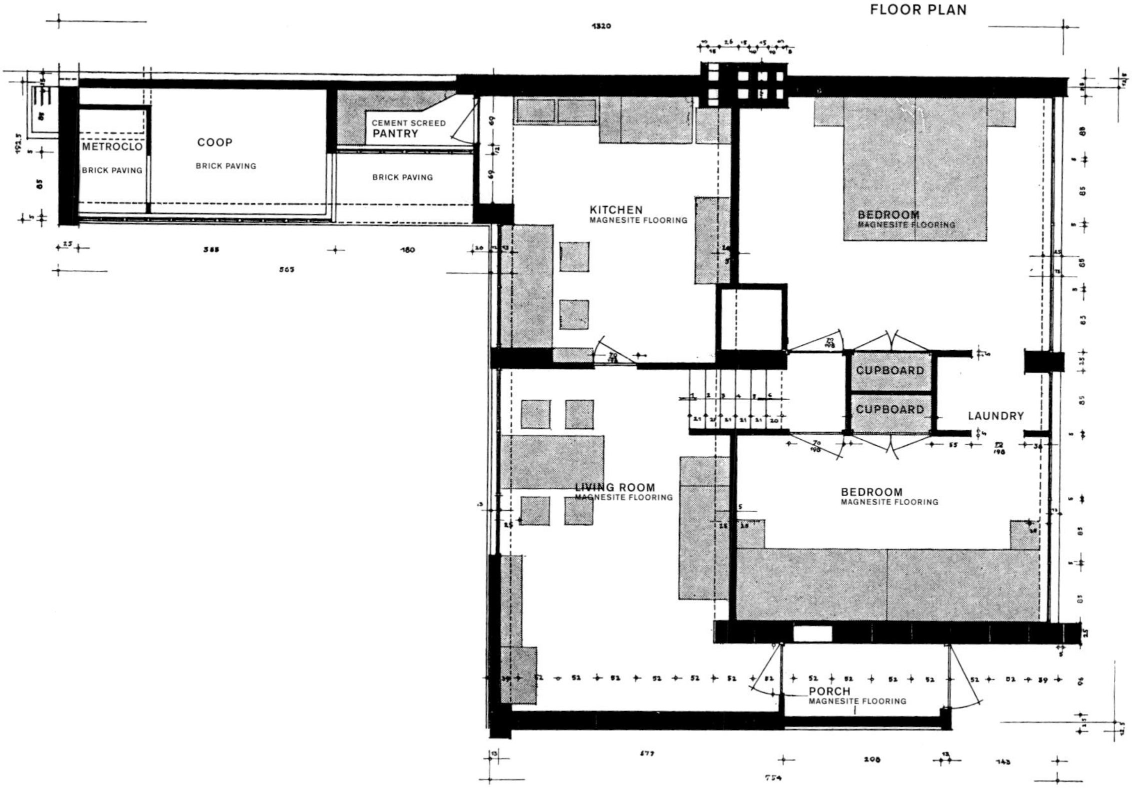


**fig. 154** dessau-törten estate
1928-type ground-floor and upstairs floor plan

**fig. 155** **dessau-törten estate**
plan for rational setup of the construction site
1926 construction phase

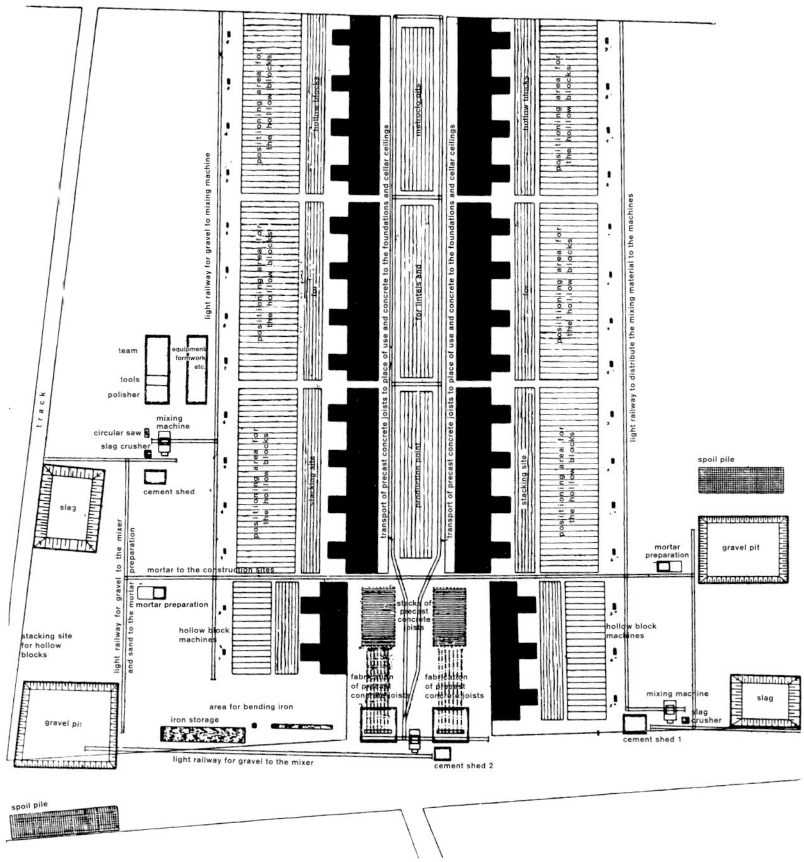


the most primitive macroeconomic fact is that our needs can be satisfied more economically, i.e. with less outlay of money, labor and materials, by constantly improving organization. this urge led to the machine, to the division of labor, to rationalization; concepts that have become indispensable to our economy and are just as important for construction as for all other branches of human activity.

**fig. 156** **dessau-törten estate**
organized construction site, 1926 construction phase according to plan in fig. 155

photo jué / dessau

the large construction site is the main prerequisite for rationalization. due to its scale, there is greater scope to deploy specially trained teams, and general expenses for management, supervision and machinery can be better spread over the entire project than in the case of small-scale construction projects.

**fig. 157** **dessau-törten estate**
timetable for skeleton construction in 1926 construction phase

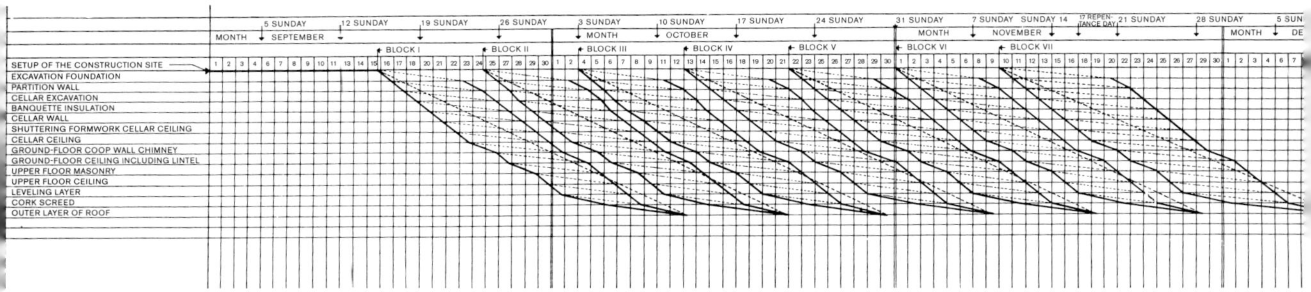


printing block bauhaus

implementing rationalization on the entire construction area in keeping with the plan would bring about such enormous savings that sufficient funds would be released to finally overcome the housing shortage.

there is ultimately only one purpose to all mechanization, to relieve human beings from material work to satisfy their essential needs, leaving their minds and hands free for higher matters. if mechanization were an end in itself, then the most crucial, vitally full human nature, the individual, the indivisible, would wither away to a form of partial nature. the roots of the struggle between the old culture of craftsmanship and the new culture of machines are to be found here. it is inevitable that the new age will develop a new, organic working unit made up of craftsmanship and machinery.

**fig. 158 dessau-törten estate**
rotating tower crane for moving the precast concrete joists for the ceiling and the reinforced concrete beams (1927)

photo baubüro gropius

**fig. 159** **dessau-törten estate**
rotating tower crane while moving 5–6 precast concrete joists for the ceiling (top and middle) or one reinforced concrete beam (bottom)

humboldt-film / berlin

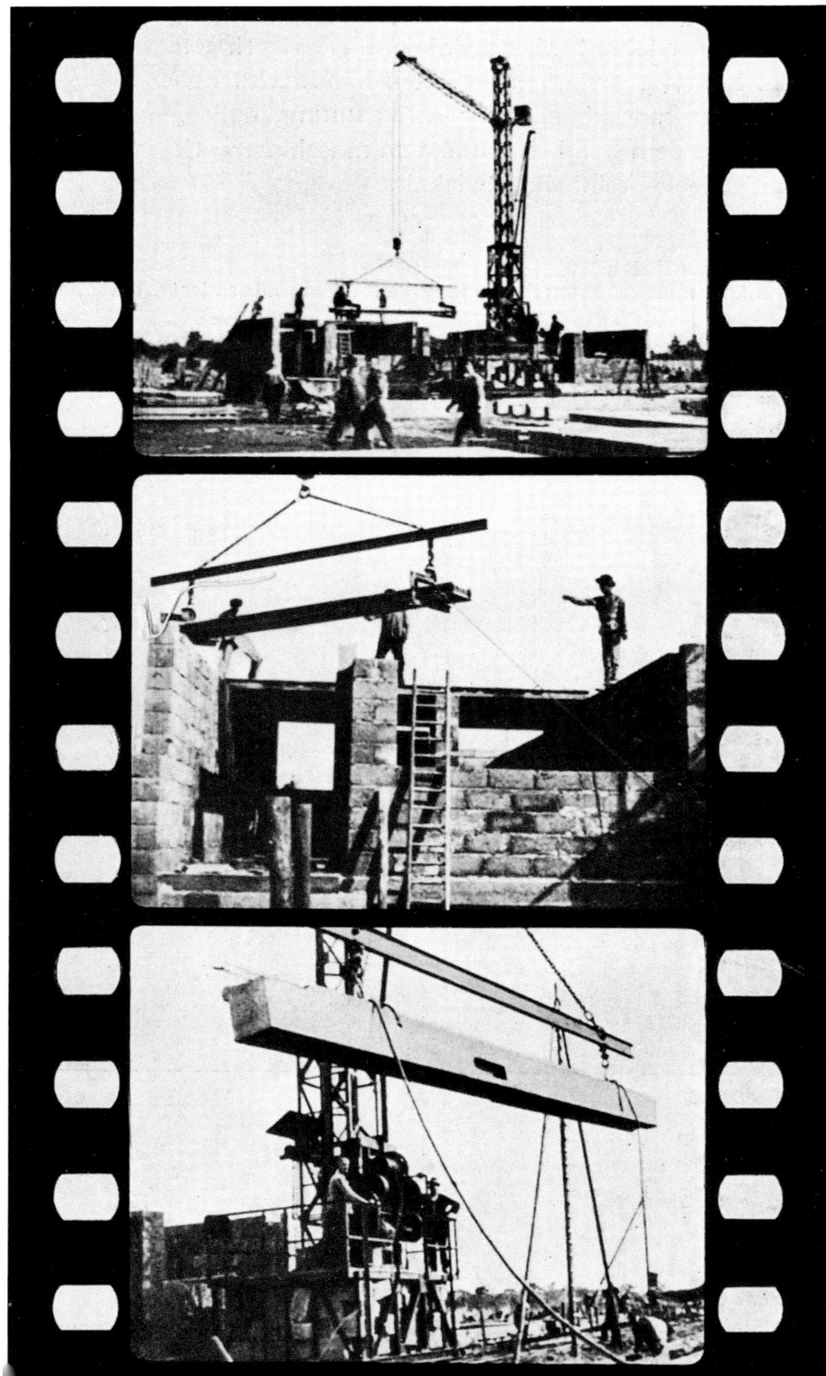

**fig. 160** dessau-törten estate
rotating tower crane moving a reinforced concrete ancillary support beam

humboldt-film / berlin

photo baubüro gropius

**fig. 161** **dessau-törten estate**
rotating tower crane positioning the load-bearing joists above the ground floor, 1928

**fig. 162** dessau-törten estate photo wedekind / dessau
1927-type construction system before installation of the non-load-bearing wall panels (road side)

the most essential feature of the new construction technique is that the functions of the walls that enclose the building are deconstructed, i.e. all of the walls are no longer erected as load-bearing components of the building, as was previously the case with the masonry house, but instead the entire building load is carried by a load-bearing skeleton frame in steel or concrete, and savings on load-bearing mass are made by using higher-quality materials, such as steel and concrete, while the walls between the supports are constructed solely to protect against the elements — against heat and cold — and against noise disturbance. in order to achieve the greatest possible savings in weight and mass to be transported, these non-load-bearing wall sections, which merely enclose the space, are to be made from thinner construction units of higher-quality material, e.g. lightweight concrete units.

just as modern industrially manufactured construction materials have evolved and attained greater precision in their properties, construction methods will also move closer to economic industrial processes, i.e. the aim will be to break down architectural structures into parts no longer produced on the construction site but mass-produced in stationary workshops, allowing these parts now to be assembled in variable compositions — the modular system on a large scale — in a dry-assembly process on the construction site, irrespective of season and weather.

**fig. 163** **dessau-törten estate**
1927-type construction system before inserting the non-load-bearing wall panels (on the right, garden side)

photo baubüro gropius

photo baubüro gropius

**fig. 164** dessau-törten estate

brick infill for the non-load-bearing wall panels, made of slag concrete panels on the interior and thermally insulating cellular concrete panels on the exterior.

At the same time, the square concrete frames are also placed to hold the staircase glazing.
1927—1928 construction phase.

**fig. 165** **dessau-törten estate**
before plastering, the tamped terrazzo windowsills are positioned
1928 construction phase

photo baubüro gropius

photo baubüro gropius

**fig. 166** dessau-törten estate
suspending the steel window frames and steel door frames before adding brick infill to the non-load-bearing wall panels

there is no question that for many sections of the population, over and above economic issues, the single-family home and garden, despite being more expensive and more difficult to run, offer essential values for residents' family life, especially for children, and that, therefore, wherever there is a real need for single-family homes, progress must be made on planned construction of this form of housing, even if the economic difficulties in executing this housing type are greater than for the apartment block, which, in its new improved form, will, of course, retain its value for urban districts.

**fig. 167 dessau-törten estate**
balconies and gardens at the rear of the rows of houses. 1927

photo baubüro gropius

photo baubüro gropius

**fig. 168** dessau-törten estate
balcony and workplace at the rear of the rows of houses. 1926

**fig. 169** dessau-törten estate
living room. inexpensive mass-produced furniture 1926
chairs: m. breuer

photo bimpage / dessau

photo consemüller / bauhaus

**fig. 170** **dessau-törten estate**
entrance
front door in steel frame. glass bricks

**fig. 171** dessau-törten estate
kitchen with fittings, 1926

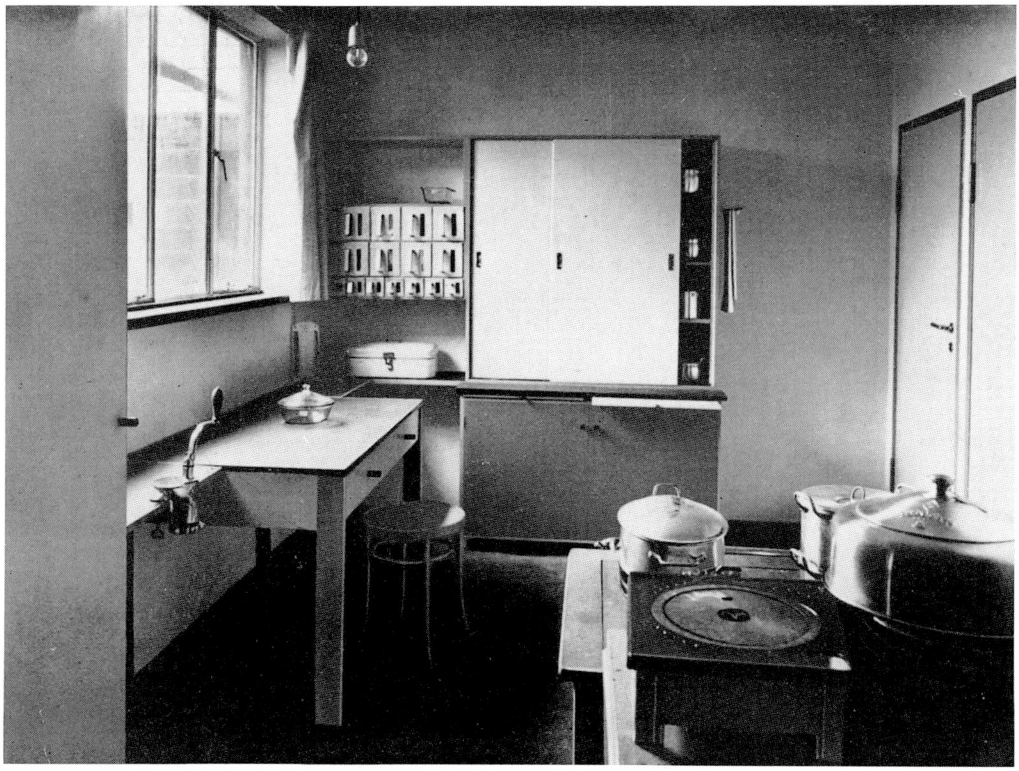

photo wedekind / dessau

photo wedekind / dessau

**fig. 172** dessau-törten estate
scullery with fittings. 1926

sink and sit-down bathtub in white terrazzo. shared pivoting tap, folding worktop above the tub. junkers gas-fired water heater.

**fig. 173** dessau-törten estate
1927-type houses

photo muche

photo muche

**fig. 174** **dessau-törten estate**
1927-type houses

**fig. 175** **dessau-törten estate**
houses of the improved 1927-type. 1928 construction phase

photo baubüro gropius

photo muche

**fig. 176** dessau-törten estate
1927-type houses

**fig. 177 dessau-törten estate**
1927-type house / garden side

a proper sense of tradition is not based on intentional, reclusive volition, but on that which is shared, the standard that is capable of satisfying many people, that has the highest level of content, the greatest quality. such dense content can only be achieved if new and powerful technical means are used, with the associated outlay only proving worthwhile through replication. devising standardized types calls for the most intensive and most radical work, if it is to prove its worth and persist, the problem of an object and its production must be thought through to the last detail, also with a view to the long term, that is how it becomes the traditional standard, because only the better is the enemy of the good.

photo baubüro gropius

photo baubüro gropius

**fig. 178** **dessau-törten estate**
1928-type houses, garden side with coop extensions and chicken runs

the chaotic lack of uniformity in our homes demonstrates the degree to which our ideas are blurred when it comes to housing that is appropriate for people today. most citizens of civilized peoples have similar needs for housing and living standards. residential accommodation is therefore a matter of mass needs. just as it would no longer occur nowadays to 90% of the population to have their shoes made to measure, as they instead purchase off-the-shelf products that satisfy most individual needs as a result of fine-tuned manufacturing methods, in the future individuals will be able to order the housing that suits them from the warehouse. a fundamental reorganization of the entire building industry, entailing moving toward an industrial approach, is the most important requirement for a modern solution of the problem. this must be approached simultaneously from three different angles: in terms of macroeconomic organization, from a technical and from a creative point of view. all three areas are interdependent. only acting simultaneously in all three areas will lead to success.

**fig. 179** dessau-törten estate
1928-type houses

photo baubüro gropius

**fig. 180** dessau-törten estate
1928-type houses, entrance side

the fully equipped house, available off-the-shelf, will soon become a principal industrial product. implementing a response to the comprehensive problem, however, requires determined joint action by national and local authorities, experts and consumers. the large constructors' organizations, states, local authorities, major industrial players have a duty to finance the requisite experiments that must precede housing production: public experimental sites with public funding support are urgently needed. just as industry subjects every object it reproduces to countless tests in systematic preliminary work, involving salespeople, technicians and artists alike, until its "standardized type" is found, the production of standardized construction components also requires systematic experimental work in generous cooperation between economic, industrial and artistic forces.

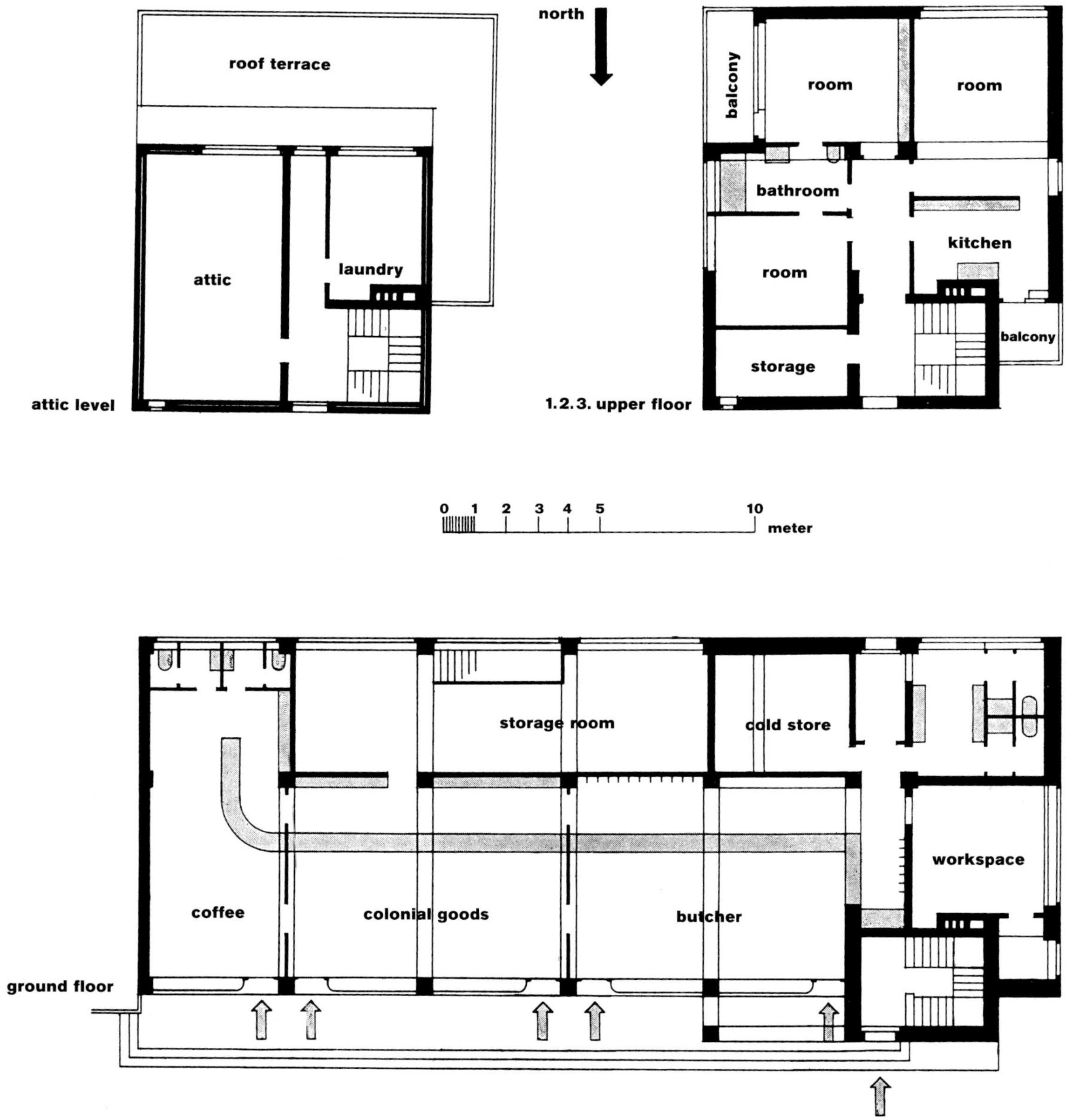


**figs. 181—183** dessau-törten estate
floor plan of the ground floor and the upper floors of the building of the konsumverein für dessau und umgegend
in the flat-roofed building: butcher, colonial goods store and café
in the tower: three apartments (3 rooms, bathroom and kitchen)

photo theis / dessau

**fig. 184** dessau-törten estate
south view of the building of the konsumverein für dessau und umgegend

**fig. 185** dessau-törten estate
northeast view of the building of the konsumverein für dessau und umgegend

photo theis / dessau

photo theis / dessau

**fig. 186** **dessau-törten estate**
center of the estate with east view of the building of the konsumverein für dessau und umgegend

the idea of rationalization, which springs from the economic activities of nations, has become a great intellectual movement in the civilized world. it has led to a changed attitude toward life, which unleashes new creative forces.

the profundity of this idea lies in its objective of establishing a productive relationship between the economic actions of the individual human being and the good of the whole, moving beyond the notion of economic profitability for individuals or particular companies. this broader interpretation of the idea of rationalization — ratio-reason — which touches on human community life, also becomes the basis of modern building concepts. for the human dwelling, the container of life, the cell of the larger community structure of the street, the city, is a complex element, with diverse functions that can only be bound together and formed into a unity by the force of reason in the higher sense of the term.

it would be erroneous to believe that the aim of rationalizing the construction industry is solely to improve existing building production economically but not in social terms. rationalization is not a mechanical order! come what may, we must not forget creativity as a result of the rational!

**employment office dessau**
**built in 1928/1929**
**architect: walter gropius**

as a consequence of industry's efforts to rationalize the production of goods, the labor market will constantly have to deal with unemployment. after the war, in order to speed up labor exchange, supply and demand, the reich took on the role of

**placing people in work.**

the buildings provisionally used as labor exchanges soon proved to be inadequate. a new type had to be created for this kind of building. the city of dessau took the initiative and in 1927 invited tenders for a semiclosed competition for an

**employment office**

in dessau. my design was selected for execution, was begun in may 1928 and in june 1929 the employment office was able to move in.

the essential issue in this

**remit**

concerned finding a type of floor plan (see fig. 188) that would meet the special requirements of this architectural genre, namely to manage the task of finding employment for as many individuals as possible looking for work in various fields with as few public officials as possible. this requirement gave rise to the semicircular configuration of the floor plan, which allows the large waiting rooms — divided into segments according to professional groups — to be arranged around the periphery, while the individual consultation rooms are located beyond them toward the interior. this solution also has the additional advantage that the fluctuating spatial requirements for the consultation rooms for men and women can be met by varying the space available by sliding the cupboards separating the rooms in the inner section. as a result of the semicircular shape, the lighting of the internal rooms was solved with the help of concentrically arranged rings of sheds, with the function of the shed-roof skylights essentially limited to letting light into the building thanks to installation of a mechanical ventilation and air extraction system (see fig. 194).

the two-story administrative wing, which is on the whole not accessible to the public, is adjacent to the semicircular low-rise building.

**the realization**

the low-rise building is a steel frame construction. all of the masonry is in leather-colored clinker bricks, the flat roof of the administrative wing is covered with a tar and gravel roof on cork screed. all windows have steel profiles. the walls of the publicly accessible rooms are clad with glazed clinker bricks. the floors of the inner and administration rooms are in natural-colored magnesite screed, the waiting rooms are in terrazzo with brass dividing strips. the bauhaus carpentry workshop supplied the furniture, the bauhaus metal workshop supplied the lighting and the bauhaus mural workshop took charge of the color design for all the rooms. the building covers 1555 square meters of built-up area and contains 7461 cubic meters of enclosed space. the cost, including all ancillary costs, was 297950 rm, or 39.9 rm per cubic meter of enclosed space.

photo theis / dessau

**fig. 187** **employment office dessau**
northwest view with the entrances around the periphery for various professions
putty-free overhead glazing for the inclined surfaces in the shed-roof sections

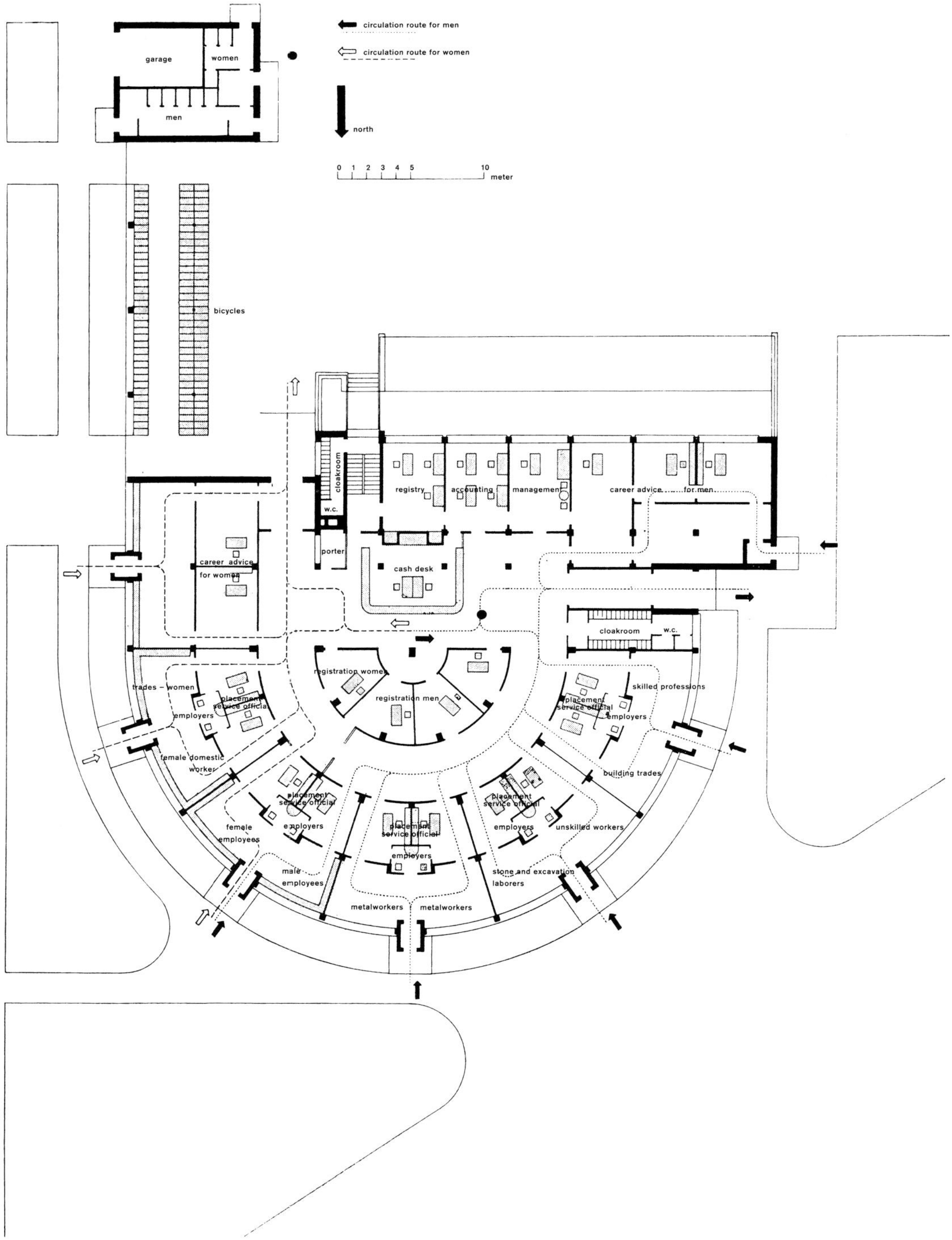


**fig. 188** **employment office dessau**
ground-floor floor plan
single-level arrangement of the main facilities to avoid congestion on stairs

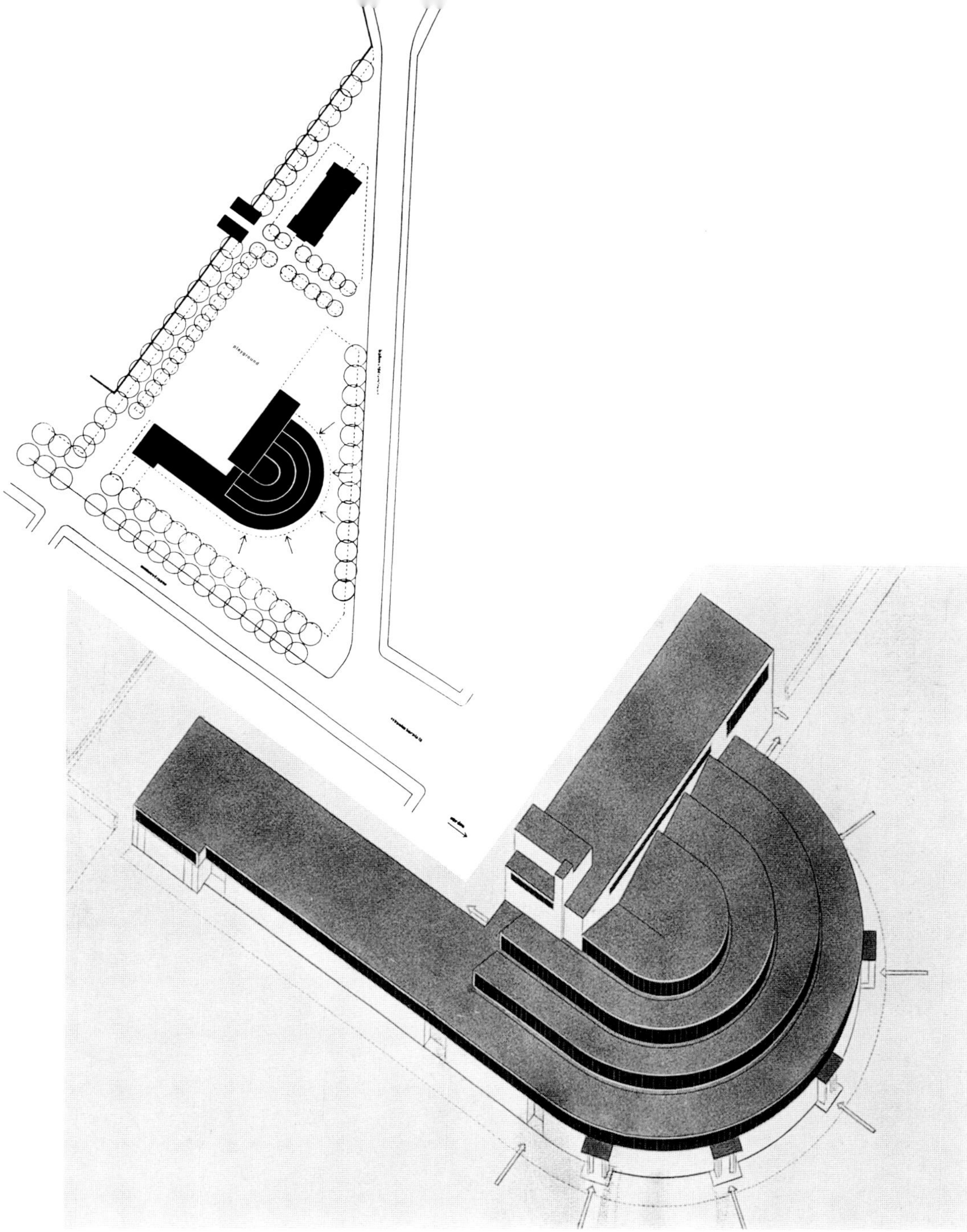

**fig. 189** employment office dessau
site plan

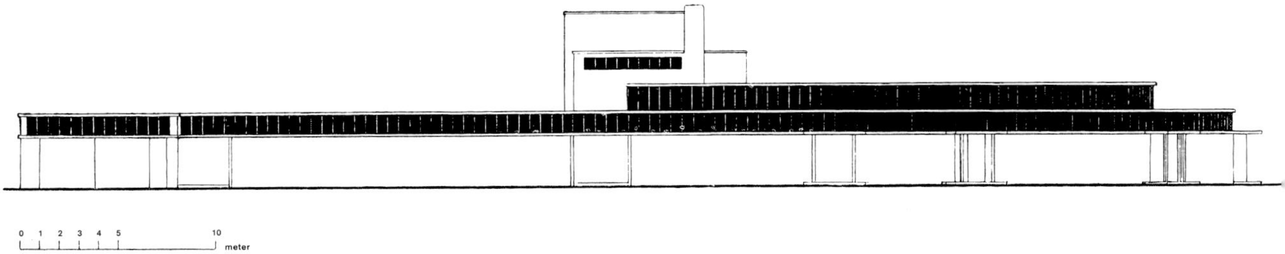


**fig. 190** employment office dessau
east view

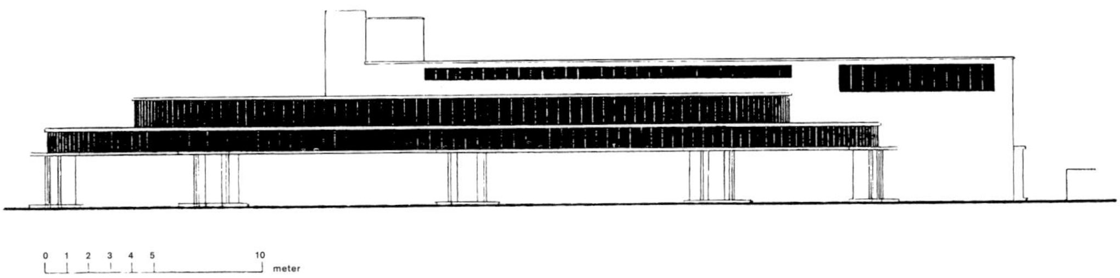


**fig. 191** employment office dessau
north view

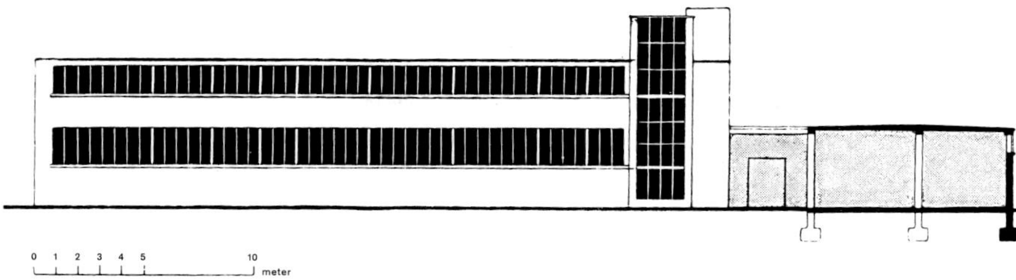


**fig. 192** employment office dessau
south view

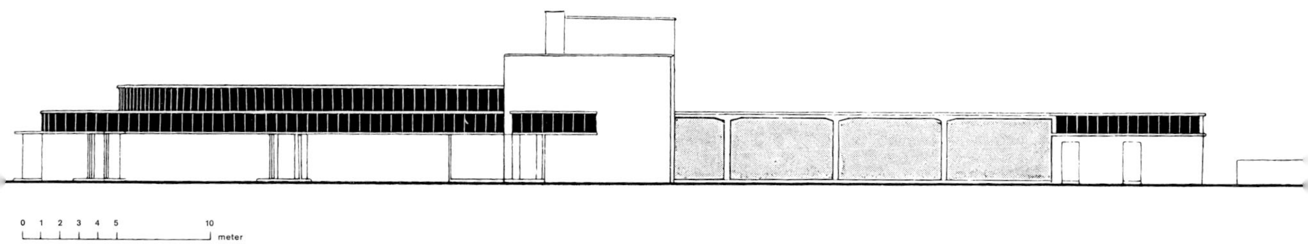


**fig. 193** employment office dessau
west view

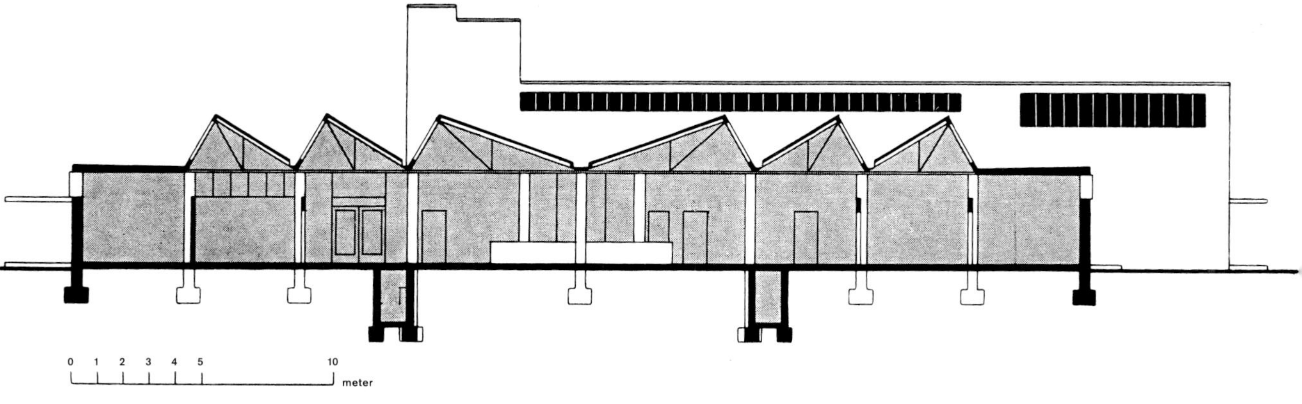


**fig. 194** employment office dessau
east-west section through the shed building

**fig. 195** **employment office dessau**
iron skeleton of the semicircular shed building

photo theis / dessau

photo theis / dessau

**fig. 196** **employment office dessau**
iron skeleton of the semicircular shed building
assembly of the purlins

**fig. 197** employment office dessau
cash desk in the center of the shed building

photo theis / dessau

photo theis / dessau

**fig. 198** **employment office dessau**
central pillar in the core of the shed building, on the right the cashier's payment desk

**fig. 199** **employment office dessau**
inner corridor in the shed building
walls: white glazed facing bricks
false ceiling: ribbed glass

photo theis / dessau

photo theis / dessau

**fig. 200** employment office dessau
central pillar in the core of the shed building

**fig. 201** **employment office dessau**
southwest view of the administrative building. bicycle shed and w. c. in the background

photo theis / dessau

photo theis / dessau

**fig. 202** **employment office dessau**
south view of the administrative building and staircase
on the right exit for female job seekers

**fig. 203 employment office dessau**
north view of the shed building with the entrances around the periphery for the various occupations

the profession of architect aims to be a unifying organizer that, starting from social ideas of life, i.e. ideas in the interest of the community, must compile solutions to all scientific, technical, economic and design problems of building and, in collaboration with numerous specialists and workers, merge them in a planned manner into a unified work.

photo theis / dessau

# list of illustrations

# bauhausbücher

schriftleitung: walter gropius
l. moholy-nagy

| | | | abbildungen | steif brosch. | i. leinen geb. |
|---|---|---|---|---|---|
| 1 | **walter gropius,** | internationale architektur<br>sechste auflage<br>auswahl der besten neuzeitlichen architekturwerke | 96 | mk. 5 | mk. 7 |
| 2 | **paul klee,** | pädagogisches skizzenbuch zweite auflage<br>aus seinem unterricht am bauhaus mit selbst gezeichneten textillustrationen | 87 | mk. 5 | mk. 7 |
| 3 | **ein versuchshaus des bauhauses** | neue wohnkultur; neue techniken des hausbaues | 61 | vergriffen | |
| 4 | **die bühne im bauhaus** | teoretisches und praktisches aus einer modernen teaterwerkstatt | 42<br>3 farbtafeln | vergriffen | |
| 5 | **piet mondrian,** | neue gestaltung<br>forderungen der neuen gestaltung für alle gebiete künstlerischen schaffens | | vergriffen | |
| 6 | **theo van doesburg,** | grundbegriffe der neuen gestaltenden kunst<br>versuch einer neuen ästetik | 32 | vergriffen | |
| 7 | **neue arbeiten der bauhauswerkstätten** | praktische beispiele neuzeitlicher wohnungseinrichtung | 107<br>4 farbtafeln | vergriffen | |
| 8 | **l. moholy-nagy,** | malerei, fotografie, film<br>fünfte auflage.<br>die probleme der neuen optischen gestaltung | 100 | mk. 7 | mk. 9 |
| 9 | **kandinsky,** | punkt und linie zu fläche<br>zweite auflage<br>beitrag zur analyse der malerischen elemente | 127<br>1 vierfarbendruck | mk. 12 | mk. 15 |
| 10 | **j. j. p. oud,** | holländische architektur. fünfte auflage<br>zusammenfassung teoretischer und praktischer erkenntnis auf dem gebiete der architektur | 55 | mk. 7 | mk. 9.50 |
| 11 | **kasimir malewitsch,** | die gegestandslose welt<br>die geschichte und begründung des russischen suprematismus | 92 | mk. 6 | mk. 8 |
| 12 | **walter gropius,** | bauhausbauten dessau<br>bauhausgebäude, bauhauswohnungen, siedlung törten, konsumverein, arbeitsamt | 203 | mk. 15 | mk. 18 |
| 13 | **albert gleizes,** | kubismus<br>die geschichte des kubismus | 47 | mk. 7 | mk. 9 |
| 14 | **l. moholy-nagy,** | von material zu architektur<br>der weg zum erlebnis von material, plastik und architektur | 209 | mk. 12 | mk. 15 |

**albert langen verlag**
**münchen / hubertusstraße 27**

At LARS MÜLLER PUBLISHERS the following titles are available in English translation and original design

**Bauhausbücher**

**1 International Architecture** by Walter Gropius
ISBN 978-3-03778-584-3
**2 Pedagogical Sketchbook** by Paul Klee
ISBN 978-3-03778-585-0
**3 A Bauhaus Experimental House** by Adolf Meyer
ISBN 978-3-03778-627-7
**4 The Theater of the Bauhaus** by Oskar Schlemmer
ISBN 978-3-03778-628-4
**5 New Design** by Piet Mondrian
ISBN 978-3-03778-586-7
**6 Principles of Neo-Plastic Art** by Theodor van Doesburg
ISBN 978-3-03778-629-1
**7 New Works from the Bauhaus Workshops** by Walter Gropius
ISBN 978-3-03778-630-7
**8 Painting, Photography, Film** by László Moholy-Nagy
ISBN 978-3-03778-587-4
**9 Point and Line to Plane** by Wassily Kandinsky
ISBN 978-3-03778-662-8
**10 Dutch Architecture** by Jacobus Johannes Pieter Oud
ISBN 978-3-03778-663-5
**11 The Non-objective World** by Kasimir Malevich
ISBN 978-3-03778-664-2
**12 Bauhaus Buildings Dessau** by Walter Gropius
ISBN 978-3-03778-665-9
**13 Cubism** by Albert Gleizes
ISBN 978-3-03778-666-6
**14 From Material to Architecture** by László Moholy-Nagy
ISBN 978-3-03778-667-3

**bauhaus journal 1926–1931**
Facsimile edition with commentary
ISBN 978-3-03778-588-1, English
ISBN 978-3-03778-594-2, German

**State Bauhaus in Weimar 1919–1923**
Facsimile edition with commentary
ISBN 978-3-03778-623-9, English
ISBN 978-3-03778-620-8, German

www.lars-mueller-publishers.com

# Walter Gropius
# Bauhaus Buildings Dessau
## Bauhausbücher 12 (1930)

It will soon be 100 years since Walter Gropius and László Moholy-Nagy made the grand gesture of initiating and publishing the *Bauhausbücher* series. Their intention to document and disseminate in book form the New Design philosophy in all areas of its application testifies to the enthusiasm that prevailed at the Bauhaus. However, only a quarter of the planned titles had been published by 1930. Political turmoil and war thwarted the further expansion of the series. The original editions are almost impossible to find today.

The goal of my initiative is to gradually make the fourteen *Bauhausbücher* available again in a form true to the originals and–in some cases for the first time–in English translation. With this project I am fulfilling my own bibliophile passion and my conviction that there is no future without a past. Only a solid knowledge of history can open up perspectives on how we can take advantage of the insights gleaned by modernism while also transcending them.

Lars Müller

The *Bauhausbücher* in this edition are designed to resemble as closely as possible the German originals from the 1920s. The typographical layout and distinguishing elements were imitated, and the look of the lead typefaces used at the time was simulated as closely as possible using today's digital technology. A concession had to be made in the choice of paper, however. The pulp used one hundred years ago with its high wood content naturally led to a yellowish paper. We assume that at the time the designers chose the whitest paper available and have therefore selected a white paper in common use today for reprinting the *Bauhausbücher.* For the cover, embossing and jacket design of our series, we have opted for a unified interpretation of the historical German book originals.

With the aim of raising the profile of the Bauhaus at home and abroad, in 1923 Walter Gropius and his newly appointed colleague László Moholy-Nagy–an artist already well versed in both the design and the targeted use of media–conceived the idea of a series of books. Over the next three years, they planned altogether fifty-four titles by different authors on a wide variety of subjects, in slim volumes that could be quickly produced. Ranging from natural sciences, literature, politics and religion to almost all the "isms" of art, the series encompassed a spectrum testifying to little short of a utopian vision (one of the proposed volumes was indeed titled *Utopisches*): to forge a connection, in terms of content, between the entire phenomena of the modern world and the avant-garde school, and to harness this knowledge for the future design of every sphere of daily life. Due to financial problems, the first eight books in this ambitious program only appeared in 1925, published by the Albert Langen Verlag. A further four volumes followed in the years up to 1928, while Gropius and Moholy-Nagy were still at the Bauhaus, and even after their departure two more also appeared under their editorship up to 1930. The two subsequent directors of the school, Hannes Meyer and Ludwig Mies van der Rohe, did not continue the *Bauhausbücher*. According to the original publicity leaflet of 1925, the fourteen published volumes in the series examine "artistic, scientific and technical issues ... from the point of view of their mutual relation." Six of the teachers at the Bauhaus–Walter Gropius, László Moholy-Nagy, Paul Klee, Adolf Meyer, Oskar Schlemmer and Wassily Kandinsky–authored nine books on their respective theoretical and educational approaches and on Bauhaus products; the remaining volumes focused on trends in art closely akin to the Bauhaus. Available in both paperback and a linen binding, the editions of around 3,000 copies usually sold out quickly and were often printed a second time. Despite the different design of their covers, the volumes are recognizable as a series thanks to their uniform format, abundance of illustrations, and their distinctive design and layout by Moholy-Nagy, characterized by striking contrasts of blank space and sans serif font, as well as by letters and graphic elements deployed for visual effect. With their compelling interplay of content and form, the *Bauhausbücher* are still today considered milestones of avant-garde book production.

Astrid Bähr
Bauhaus-Archiv / Museum für Gestaltung, Berlin

# About *Bauhaus Buildings Dessau*

In *Bauhaus Buildings Dessau* Walter Gropius did not merely present a comprehensive documentation of his architectural legacy from 1925 to 1929 in this up-and-coming industrial city, but also self-confidently emphasized that these buildings would serve as exemplary models for future architecture. At the same time, he picked up on the previous *Bauhausbücher* that he had conceived: While in the first volume, *International Architecture*, he had articulated a fundamental defense of modern architecture and its forms and typologies in Europe and North America, *A Bauhaus Experimental House* presented the first residential building created by the Bauhaus as a model of mass production methods in the construction sector. In the present volume, he demonstrated the full breadth of his theoretical considerations as implemented in the architecture built in Dessau, the city to which the Bauhaus had relocated in 1925, having left Weimar after the Free State of Thuringia withdrew its political and financial support. Fritz Hesse, Mayor of Dessau, had also tipped the scales in Dessau's favor by alluding to the prospect of numerous building contracts for the Bauhaus. Within just four years, the Bauhaus school building and four houses for faculty members were constructed here, along with the municipal employment office and the Törten residential estate, comprising four different building typologies and sections. This broad spectrum served to demonstrate the fundamental reform of architecture that had been proclaimed when the school was founded in 1919, a blow was struck for *Neues Bauen* [New Building], while the publication also spread awareness of the school's potential thanks to the new form of education it pursued.

However, it was not until 1930 that *Bauhaus Buildings Dessau* was published as the last volume in the series, two years after Gropius had resigned as Bauhaus Director, subsequently leaving the city and being succeeded by Hannes Meyer. Only the school building and the *Meisterhäuser* (Bauhaus masters' apartments) were constructed during Gropius's time as director and even these projects were implemented by Gropius's architecture studio, with the exception of the interior design work by the Bauhaus workshops, as the Bauhaus did not launch its own architecture class until 1927. Nevertheless, Gropius declared all these buildings–including the Törten estate and the employment office, which were only constructed after his departure–to be *Bauhaus buildings*: an astute move to expand the number and significance of the buildings realized at the school and thus lay claim to the entire Bauhaus even after his departure.

In the projects presented in images and text in *Bauhaus Buildings Dessau,* Gropius demonstrated mastery of no less than four different architectural challenges,

At Lars Müller Publishers, the complete 14-volume series of the *Bauhausbücher* is available:

**1 Walter Gropius, *International Architecture,*** 1925 (2019),
ISBN 978-3-03778-584-3
**2 Paul Klee, *Pedagogical Sketchbook,*** 1925 (2019),
ISBN 978-3-03778-585-0
**3 Adolf Meyer, *A Bauhaus Experimental House,*** 1925 (2020),
ISBN 978-3-03778-627-7
**4 Oskar Schlemmer, *The Theater of the Bauhaus,*** 1925 (2020),
ISBN 978-3-03778-628-4
**5 Piet Mondrian, *New Design,*** 1925 (2019),
ISBN 978-3-03778-586-7
**6 Theo van Doesburg, *Principles of Neo-Plastic Art,*** 1925 (2020),
ISBN 978-3-03778-629-1
**7 Walter Gropius, *New Works from the Bauhaus Workshops,*** 1925 (2020),
ISBN 978-3-03778-630-7
**8 László Moholy-Nagy, *Painting, Photography, Film,*** 1925 (2019),
ISBN 978-3-03778-587-4
**9 Wassily Kandinsky, *Point and Line to Plane,*** 1926 (2021),
ISBN 978-3-03778-662-8
**10 Jacobus Johannes Pieter Oud, *Dutch Architecture,*** 1926 (2021),
ISBN 978-3-03778-663-5
**11 Kasimir Malevich, *The Non-objective World,*** 1927 (2021),
ISBN 978-3-03778-664-2
**12 Walter Gropius, *Bauhaus Buildings Dessau,*** 1930 (2021),
ISBN 978-3-03778-665-9
**13 Albert Gleizes, *Cubism,*** 1928 (2021),
ISBN 978-3-03778-666-6
**14 László Moholy-Nagy, *From Material to Architecture,*** 1929 (2021),
ISBN 978-3-03778-667-3

**bauhaus journal 1926–1931**
Facsimile edition with commentary (2019)
ISBN 978-3-03778-588-1, English
ISBN 978-3-03778-594-2, German

**State Bauhaus in Weimar 1919–1923**
Facsimile edition with commentary (2019)
ISBN 978-3-03778-623-9, English
ISBN 978-3-03778-620-8, German

www.lars-mueller-publishers.com/bauhaus

Image credits:
Cover, 4–6, 8–13, 15, 19–21, 23, 29–32, 35, 36, 39, 50, 60, 61, 64, 65, 68, 74, 76–87, 89, 90, 95–102, 104, 106–8, 110, 112–14, 116–18, 120, 122–31, 133–41, 143, 144, 146–55, 157, 158, 161, 163–68, 173–83, 188–94:
Bauhaus-Archiv Berlin / VG Bild-Kunst
25, 27, 40, 43, 46, 62, 63: © 2021, ProLitteris, Zurich
26, 51–59, 69, 72, 73, 132, 170: © Stephan Consemüller
34, 41, 42, 44, 45, 47: © Estate of T. Lux Feininger
66, 67, 70, 71: © Nachlass Walter Peterhans, Museum Folkwang, Essen
184–87, 195–203: © Emil Theis / Andreas Elze
We have endeavored to identify all copyright holders. Should despite our intensive research any person entitled to rights have been overlooked, they are kindly requested to contact the publisher.

**Walter Gropius**
**Bauhaus Buildings Dessau**
Bauhausbücher 12 (1930)
First English Edition (2021)

Editor: Lars Müller
Foreword and commentary: Astrid Bähr
Project management: Miriam Eickhoff
Translation: Helen Ferguson
Translation (leaflet): Jennifer Taylor, Karen Williams, Helen Ferguson
Proofreading: Keonaona Peterson
Typesetting and production: Esther Butterworth
Lithography, printing and binding: DZA Druckerei zu Altenburg, Germany
Paper: Infinity Silk, 135 gsm
Typefaces: Akzidenz-Grotesk Pro, FuturaBT, GT Eesti Text, Neue moderne Grotesk, Grot10



The German original *Bauhausbauten Dessau* was published in 1930 by Albert Langen Verlag München.



Lars Müller Publishers is supported by the Swiss Federal Office of Culture with a structural contribution for the years 2021–2024.

Lars Müller Publishers
Zurich, Switzerland
www.lars-mueller-publishers.com

ISBN 978-3-03778-665-9

Distributed in North America by ARTBOOK | D.A.P.
www.artbook.com

Printed in Germany

**We thank the Bauhaus-Archiv / Museum für Gestaltung, Berlin, for their advice and support.**

**Published with the generous support of the Rudolf-August Oetker-Stiftung.**

all of which he held to entail manifestations of his conviction that construction means "designing life processes." Over and above an emphasis on utilizing new materials, new technical designs and economic efficiency, Gropius's text also underlined the focus on function that is apparent in all the Dessau buildings: the main school building with the five different areas, separated by function, namely the workshop building, the teaching space for Dessau Technical College and wing with the residential studios, as well as the connecting section housing the administrative offices, and the auditorium and canteen; the *Meisterhäuser*, with floor plans focused on organizing the flow of activities in the studio and home; the Törten residential estate, reflecting Gropius's goal of promoting large-scale production of housing for workers through economic mass construction methods; or the innovative employment office with its semicircular floor plan designed to optimize administrative procedures. This emphasis on the functional aspects of construction and on aligning all architecture to a community's needs as fundamental facets of the Bauhaus's activities is a consistent leitmotif throughout Gropius's publication. Almost as a counterpoint to the school's Expressionist-tinged founding manifesto published eleven years earlier, *Bauhaus Buildings Dessau* now represents a modernism based on novel technology and simultaneously directed towards society, thus embodying the true legacy of Gropius's Bauhaus transposed into material form.

Within the *Bauhausbücher* series, László Moholy-Nagy's cover design is particularly striking: Like an architect's blueprint, the high-angle perspectival view of the Törten estate is superimposed over the dust jacket, where the title stands out in the recently developed *Futura black* typeface. The lavish illustrations, including 35 architectural plans and 197 photographs, are particularly carefully conceived. Gropius, a documentarian par excellence of his projects, drew on photographs from Bauhaus circles (Lucia Moholy, Erich Consemüller, T. Lux and Lyonel Feininger, Ise Gropius and Georg Muche) as well as from contemporary news reporting. His deft arrangement of these images guided the viewer's perception, conjuring up a real sense of experiencing the architecture in the image. In this spirit, the viewer moves in closer to the buildings, beginning with aerial shots that capture the ensemble and its configuration within the layout of the city, then proceeding to exterior shots that emphasize how it is embedded in the landscape, in many cases arranged in a sequence that offers a chance to circle around the building, and finally honing in on interior shots and close-ups of details such as the mechanisms for operating the windows or the telephone system. While photographs of the shells of the buildings illustrate the structural engineering and choice of materials, Gropius deliberately uses strips of negatives with film sequences from contemporary footage to shed light on the organizational processes involved. Shots of students eating or doing sports plunge the viewer directly into activities unfolding at the Bauhaus, capturing a sense of life at the school. It therefore comes as no surprise that *Bauhaus Buildings Dessau* still constitutes the central source in the reception of Gropius's Dessau buildings.

Astrid Bähr

**Walter Gropius**, * May 18, 1883, in Berlin; † July 5, 1969, in Boston, Massachusetts, USA. In 1903 Walter Gropius went to study architecture at Munich's Technische Hochschule (Technical University). Two years later he moved to the Technische Hochschule in Berlin-Charlottenburg, but in 1908 left without graduating and started working as a freelance architect. During World War I, Gropius was drafted into the German army and sent to the Western Front. In 1919 he formed the Staatliches Bauhaus in Weimar (Weimar State Bauhaus). In 1928 Hannes Meyer took over as Bauhaus director at Gropius's suggestion. After his departure from the school, Gropius moved to Berlin to work as an independent architect. After the National Socialists came to power, Gropius emigrated first to England and in 1937 to the USA, where he became a professor at Harvard University's Graduate School of Design in Cambridge, Massachusetts. In 1946 he cofounded The Architects Collaborative Inc. (TAC). Gropius died in 1969 in Boston, Massachusetts.

According to advertisements printed in the back of some volumes of the *Bauhausbücher* as well as in pre-order brochures elsewhere, the following further titles were planned to be published in the series, but never realized due to the events of the time:

Josef Albers, *Funktionsformen* (Functional Forms)
George Antheil, *Musico-Mechanico* (Musico-Mechanico)
Hans Arp and Tristan Tzara, *Dadaismus* (Dadaism)
Adolf Behne, *Kunst, Handwerk und Industrie* (Art, Craft and Industry)
Adolf Behne, *Russland* (Russia)
Adolf Behne and Max Burchartz / Max Burchartz, *Plastik der Gestaltungen* (Sculpture of Designs)
Max Burchartz, *Gestaltung* (Design)
Walter Gropius, *Neue Architekturdarstellung* (New Architecture Representation)
Walter Gropius, *Das flache Dach. Montierbare Typenbauten* (The Flat Roof. Mountable Type Buildings)
Raoul Hausmann, *Optophonetik* (Optophonetics)
Jane Heap, *Die neue Welt* (The New World)
Heinrich Jacoby, *Schöpferische Musikerziehung* (Creative Musical Education)
Ernő Kállai and Lajos Kassák, *Die Arbeit der MA-Gruppe / Die MA-Gruppe* (The Work of the MA Group / The MA Group)
Wassily Kandinsky, *Violett (Bühnenstück mit Einleitung und Szenerie)* (Violet [Stage Play with Introduction and Scenery])
Friedrich Kiesler, *Neue Formen der Demonstration. Die Raumstadt* (New Forms of Demonstration. The Space City)
Paul Klee, *Bildnerische Mechanik* (Pictorial Mechanics)
Le Corbusier / Le Corbusier-Saugnier [Saugnier: Amédée Ozenfant], *Über Architektur* (On Architecture)
El Lissitzky, *Reklame und Typographie* (Advertisement and Typography)
Knud Lonberg-Holm, *Über Architektur* (On Architecture)
Louis Lozowick, *Amerikanische Architektur* (American Architecture)
Filippo Tommaso Marinetti and Enrico Prampolini, *Futurismus* (Futurism)
Adolf Meyer, *Die neuen Materialen* (The New Materials)
Ludwig Mies van der Rohe, *Über Architektur* (On Architecture)
László Moholy-Nagy, *Werkarbeit der Gestaltungen* (Workmanship of Designs)
László Moholy-Nagy, *Aufbau der Gestaltungen* (Structure of Designs)
Georg Muche, *Amerika?–Europa* (America?–Europe)
Georg Muche and Richard Paulick, *Das Metall Typenhaus* (The Metal Type House)
Martin Schäfer, *Konstruktive Biologie* (Constructive Biology)
Oskar Schlemmer, *Bildermagazin der Zeit I* (Image Journal of the Time I)
Oskar Schlemmer, *Bühnenelemente* (Elements of Theater)
Joost Schmidt, *Bildermagazin der Zeit II* (Image Journal of the Time II)
Kurt Schwitters, *Merz-Buch* (Merz Book)
Mart Stam, *Das "ABC" vom Bauen* (The "ABC" of Building)
Karel Teige, *Tschechische Kunst* (Czech Art)
Theo van Doesburg, *Die Arbeit der Stijl-Gruppe / Die Stijl-Gruppe* (The Work of the De Stijl Group / The Stijl Group)
Fritz Wichert, *Expressionismus* (Expressionism)

N.N., *Architektur, Malerei, Plastik aus den Werkstätten des Bauhauses* (Architecture, Painting, Sculpture from the Bauhaus Workshops)
N.N., *Die neuen künstlichen Materialien* (The New Artificial Materials)
N.N., *Kleinwohnungen von der Architekturabteilung des* Bauhauses (Small Apartments from the Architecture Department of the Bauhaus)
N.N., *Reklame und Typographie des Bauhauses* (Advertisement and Typography of the Bauhaus)

Varying authors and titles are indicated with a slash.

Editorial note

Typographical errors from the German original were not adopted but corrected according to the current spelling. The consequent use of lowercase letters has been adopted from the German original. Floor levels are indicated in the European system, where the street level floor is called "ground floor," whereas upper floors are counted starting by first floor. The names of companies, administrative offices and street names were not translated. The abbreviation "Sietö," German, short for "Siedlung Törten," was not adopted but spelled out as "Törten Estate." Following the corrigendum in the first edition of the book ("Fig. 18 on p. 33 has been inverted by mistake in the page layout and should therefore be viewed from the upper edge of the page"), the image has been rotated by 180° for correction in this edition. In contradiction to the caption of Fig. 143 on p. 160, the units of the 1926 construction phase are missing in the plan. This has been adopted from the German original.

This book contains gender-based ascriptions that were commonplace in European society at the time of its publication. As with the decision to adhere to the original design of the *Bauhausbücher,* we resolved to translate the original wording of the texts unaltered, with full awareness of their faults. We support the ongoing discourses on equality and inclusivity and encourage our readers to engage in these important debates.